T0090685

Also by Steve Dugan

*The Nine Words: A Story of Faith,
Love & Perseverance*

GREAT NEWS FROM GOD!

STEVE DUGAN

WESTBOW
PRESS®
A DIVISION OF THOMAS NELSON
& ZONDERVAN

WestBow Press books may be ordered through booksellers or by contacting:

WestBow Press
A Division of Thomas Nelson & Zondervan
1663 Liberty Drive
Bloomington, IN 47403
www.westbowpress.com
844-714-3454

ISBN: 979-8-3850-1340-1 (sc)
ISBN: 979-8-3850-1341-8 (hc)
ISBN: 979-8-3850-1344-9 (e)

Library of Congress Control Number: 2023922711

Print information available on the last page.

WestBow Press rev. date: 11/28/2023

CONTENTS

DEDICATION

To Julie,

who has been great news from God

to me for over fifty-three years!

Foreword

If you like the Bible, you're going to love this collection of messages. They contain great news from God.

The word gospel means "good news." Of course, not everything that happened in the Bible seemed like good news when it took place.

To the people who loved Jesus, his crucifixion did not seem like good news at the time it happened. But, now we know that it was the best news the world has ever received.

This collection of messages illustrates one big thing. When we're going through tough times, we are exactly where God is most likely to speak to us. So, we must keep our eyes open and our ears alert to hear from Him.

In these messages, you'll see true examples of God bringing great news to me when I was discouraged. I didn't have to go looking for God to get the great news He had for me, either. He literally came to me from out of the blue and told me where to go in the Bible to find it. It's the most exciting thing that ever happened to me!

God told me to share this thought with you. Never be defeated by your circumstances. God has great news for you!

Steve Dugan

November 13, 2023

Mobile, Alabama

MESSAGE 1

The Burning Bush

The first time I got discouraged and questioned if God had really meant for me to write *The Nine Words*, I was just sitting in our den with my wife watching TV. From out of nowhere, I got a feeling that I should read about the burning bush. I paused the TV, got out the Bible, and read the story of the burning bush. The following passages encouraged me.

One day Moses was tending the flock of his father-in-law, Jethro, the priest of Midian. He led the flock far into the wilderness and came to Sinai, the mountain of God. There the angel of the Lord appeared to him in a blazing fire from the middle of a bush. Moses stared in amazement. Though the bush was engulfed in flames, it didn't burn up. "This is amazing," Moses said to himself.

"Why isn't the bush burning up? I must go see it."

When the Lord saw Moses coming to take a closer look, God called to him from the middle of the bush, "Moses! Moses!"

"Here I am!" Moses replied.

Exodus 3: 1-4 (NLT)

Then, God told Moses what He was calling him to do.

"Now go, for I am sending you to Pharaoh. You must lead my people Israel out of Egypt."

But Moses protested to God, "Who am I to appear before Pharaoh? Who am I to lead the people of Israel out of Egypt?"

God answered, "I will be with you. And this is your sign that I am the one who has sent you: When you have brought the people out of Egypt, you will worship God at this very mountain.”

Exodus 3:10-12 (NLT)

I saw immediately why God had put it in my mind to read about the burning bush. Moses' experience had a lot in common with my experience. We had both been minding our own business without expecting anything out of the ordinary to happen. Then, God had done something that so obviously defied the laws of nature that it got our attention, made us curious, and prepared us to hear from God.

In Moses' case, it was seeing a bush on fire but not burning up. In my case, it was being able to see right through the bodies of two girls at whom I had looked. After getting our undivided attention by performing these miracles, God spoke to both of us and told us what He wanted us to do.

God told Moses to bring the children of Israel out of Egypt. God told me, when I was just 12 years old, that the third girl I looked at, who I could not see through, was wise and that I should marry her. Neither Moses nor I knew how to go about doing what God had told us to do.

Forty years after God called Moses to do something Moses did not think he could do, God brought Moses back to the place where God had called him to see that what God had called him to do had been accomplished. Eight years after God called me to do something I did not think I could do, God brought me back within a few blocks of the place where God had called me to see that what God had called me to do had also been accomplished.

God led me to read about the burning bush to show me similarities between what happened when He called Moses and what happened when He called me.

By doing this, God relieved my discouragement and gave me the encouragement I needed. This reassured me that God really was going to use *The Nine Words* to help people.

I want to emphasize that there is nothing special about me. I believe that God is anxious to do the same things in everybody else's life that He did in mine. God is very accessible. But, I believe we have to retreat from the battles of life in order to get closer to Him.

Dear God, Thank you for noticing when I get discouraged and for giving me the encouragement I need during those times. In Jesus' name, Amen

MESSAGE 2

Elijah

Put yourself in my place and ask if my life makes any sense to you. God spoke nine words to me in 1962, when I was 12. In those nine words, He told me who I should marry and why I should marry her. I was absolutely incapable of making that happen. But, during the following eight years, God did miracle after miracle to make what He told me to do come to pass.

Then, during the Christmas holidays of 2021, I asked God what I could do in the coming year to make the money that my wife and I needed to pay our rent and our other necessary bills. The answer I received was to write the true story of the words God spoke to me when I was 12 and the miracles He did to make them come to pass.

Then, during 2022, God did miracle after miracle to provide the money we needed to live while I was working on writing that book. He also provided people to encourage me and to help me get the book published. It was published during Christmas week of 2022. I was able to surprise members of my family by giving them a copy for Christmas.

I thought the book would help a lot of people. After all, it was a true testimony about how much God cares about all of our lives and about his willingness to do miracles to help us. Since it was true and God had told me to write it, I expected that God would get it into the hands of many people who needed the encouragement that it provided. I thought that God must have an important use for it, or He wouldn't have done all those miracles that led to the book being written and published.

But, the book just lay in obscurity. Almost nobody

knew about it. It wasn't helping people the way I thought it would.

I tried everything I could think of to get it out to people, but nothing worked. Finally, I started giving copies of the book to people I knew, thinking that the people I gave it to would read it, like it, tell their friends about it, and start a chain reaction that would lead to the book becoming a success. But, most of the people to whom I gave a copy either never read it or didn't like it.

This was very discouraging to me. It just didn't make any sense. If I had written a detective novel and it was a flop, I could have just concluded that it was not a good book and moved on with my life. But, this was not a novel that I had thought up. This was my true testimony about some of the things God had done in my life. God had told me to write it, and God had done miracles to get it published.

So, I got very depressed. I started wondering how this whole project could have just fizzled out into nothing. I started wondering if the book had really been God's idea. In spite of God having spoken audibly to me and in spite of all the miracles I had witnessed, I was overcome with questions and confusion. I realized that I did not really have very strong faith after all.

Then, on another night as I sat in my chair watching TV with my wife, I got another message in my head. This second message I got was to read about Elijah.

I stopped what I was doing and picked up a Bible. I started going through it looking for the book of Elijah. I knew it had to be in The Old Testament, but I could not find it. Finally, I typed into the computer, "Where is Elijah in the Bible?" When the answer popped up, I saw why I had not been able to find the book of Elijah. There is no book of Elijah! Elijah's story is found in 1 Kings 17-19 and 2 Kings 1-2.

Naturally I was anxious to read it. I wanted to see why God had given me the message to read it. The following are some of the highlights of Elijah's story that had special meaning for me.

It starts with Elijah, apparently on his own initiative, speaking to King Ahab.

"As surely as the Lord, the God of Israel, lives—the God I serve—there will be no dew or rain during the next few years until I give the word."

Then the Lord said to Elijah, "Go to the east and hide by Kerith Brook, near where it enters the Jordan River. Drink from the brook and eat what the ravens bring you, for I have commanded them to bring you food."

1 Kings 17:1-4 (NLT)

After a while, the brook dried up.

Then the Lord said to Elijah, "Go and live in the

village of Zarephath, near the city of Sidon. I have instructed a widow there to feed you."

1 Kings 17:8-9 (NLT)

The Bible tells how Elijah stayed in the woman's house. While he was there, the woman's son died.

Then Elijah cried out to the Lord, "O Lord my God, why have you brought tragedy to this widow who has opened her home to me, causing her son to die?"

And he stretched himself over the child three times and cried out to the Lord, "O Lord my God, please let this child's life return to him." The Lord heard Elijah's prayer, and the life of the child returned, and he revived! Then Elijah brought him down from the upper room and gave him to his mother. "Look!" he said. "Your son is alive!"

Then the woman told Elijah, "Now I know for sure

that you are a man of God, and that the Lord truly speaks through you."

1 Kings 17:20-24 (NLT)

After I read these scriptures, I thought to myself, "Think about what you have just read! God spoke to Elijah. God did incredible miracles to protect Elijah from King Ahab and to provide Elijah with food to eat and a place to live. God even raised a child from the dead, when Elijah asked Him to."

Then, the reason God had told me to read about Elijah hit me like a ton of bricks! If a person who received all the miracles and answered prayers that Elijah received still panicked due to a lack of faith, then God would be telling me that I wasn't so bad for having such weak faith, myself. So, I quickly read through Elijah's story, looking to see if he ever panicked after hearing God's voice and receiving such powerful miracles, just like I did.

The Bible said the following.

Later on, in the third year of the drought, the Lord said to Elijah, "Go and present yourself to King Ahab. Tell him that I will soon send rain!" So, Elijah went to appear before Ahab. Meanwhile, the famine had become very severe in Samaria.

1 Kings 18:1-2 (NLT)

The Bible describes how Elijah met King Ahab and the followers of Baal. God did miracles to show that the God Elijah worshipped was the one true God. Finally, Elijah prayed, God made it rain, and the drought ended.

In spite of all this, King Ahab still wanted to kill Elijah.

Elijah was afraid and fled for his life, He went to Beersheba, a town in Judah, and he left his servant there. Then he went on alone into the wilderness, traveling all day. He sat down under a solitary broom tree and prayed that he might die. "I have had enough,

Lord," he said. "Take my life, for I am no better than my

ancestors who have already died."

1 Kings 19:3-4 (NLT)

That was the reason God told me to read about

Elijah! God wanted me to see that even people trying

to answer his call to serve Him, to whom He has

audibly spoken and for whom He has performed

incredible miracles, still get so severely discouraged

that they tell God that they have had enough and ask

God to let them die. My encouragement from God

was Him showing me that my discouragement did

not mean that I was on the wrong road or that I was

experiencing anything that prophets in the Bible had

not experienced. My experience and my feelings were

like Elijah's experience and like Elijah's feelings.

In spite of the fact that Elijah got so discouraged

that he told God that he had enough and asked God to let him die, the Bible says that Elijah was one of only two people who never did die. Instead, God sent a chariot of fire and horses that took Elijah to Heaven in a whirlwind. Later, in The New Testament, Jesus took three of his disciples up on a mountain, where Moses and Elijah appeared and where Jesus was transfigured, his face and clothes becoming dazzlingly bright.

God saw Elijah's depression and anxiety. But, even after seeing the weakness of Elijah, God went on to use him in even more awesome ways than He had before. This encouraged me to have hope that, in spite of how discouraging things seemed, God could still use me and achieve the things that He had told me to do.

Dear God, Thank you for being patient with me, even when you see that my faith is weak. In Jesus' name, Amen

Message 3

Samuel

Every time God gave me encouragement by having me read something specific in the Bible, I got very excited and had renewed confidence that God really was going to use the testimony He had told me to write to encourage many people. I knew that I didn't have the ability to do it. However, I believed that if I did the best I could, God would touch hearts and do miracles to make it happen. I would wake up every day looking for evidence that God was making positive things happen for the book I had written. After all, if He wasn't going to make something happen, why would He have gone to so much trouble to encourage me?

I would call book stores and ask them to carry the book on their shelves. I would call everybody I could think of to help me promote it. But, things did not go forward. In fact, I was confronted every day by the fact that things were going in reverse. New people I asked to help me promote the book refused to do it. Even worse and more depressing, some of the key people who had felt called by God to help me get the book published in 2021 no longer wanted anything to do with the book in 2022. I think this was because I bothered them so much.

I prayed about this every day. I tried to figure out what I could do to regain the friendship and help of people who had been so instrumental in helping me get the book published just a year before. My calls to most of these people went unreturned and my messages to them got no replies. I would sit down at night, after Julie had gone to bed, and read the book again to see if there was something wrong with it.

I was confused and distressed. I knew the people

who were not helping me were very good people. I didn't blame any of them. I just didn't understand why no progress was being made. I began to question the whole thing again. Could I have made all this up? I didn't think so, but I had only been 12 years old when God spoke to me, and I couldn't even remember how God's voice had sounded. How could I have possibly forgotten anything as important as that?

So, as day after day went by with no progress being made, I became more and more discouraged. Then on yet another night, as I was watching TV with my wife again, another message popped into my head. This one was, "Read about the calling of Samuel." As I had done after receiving the other messages like this, I stopped watching TV, got a Bible, and started reading.

I read that Samuel's mother, Hannah, had not been able to have a child.

Hannah was in deep anguish, crying bitterly as she

prayed to the Lord. And she made this vow: "O Lord of Heaven's Armies, if you will look upon my sorrow and answer my prayer and give me a son, then I will give him back to you. He will be yours for his entire lifetime, and as a sign that he has been dedicated to the Lord, his hair will never be cut."

1 Samuel 1:10-11 (NLT)

The Bible says that in due time Hannah had a son. After he was weaned, she took him to Eli, the priest at the Tabernacle, and left him there permanently. Then, I read what I had been looking for most, the circumstances of Samuel's calling.

Meanwhile, the boy Samuel served the Lord by assisting Eli. Now in those days messages from the Lord were very rare, and visions were quite uncommon.

One night Eli, who was almost blind by now, had gone to bed. The lamp of God had not yet gone out, and

Samuel was sleeping in the Tabernacle near the Ark of God. Suddenly the Lord called out, "Samuel!"

"Yes?" Samuel replied. "What is it?" He got up and ran to Eli. "Here I am. Did you call me?"

"I didn't call you," Eli replied. "Go back to bed." So he did.

Then the Lord called out again, "Samuel!"

Again Samuel got up and went to Eli. "Here I am. Did you call me?"

"I didn't call you, my son," Eli said. "Go back to bed."

Samuel did not yet know the Lord because he had never had a message from the Lord before. So the Lord called a third time, and once more Samuel got up and went to Eli. "Here I am. Did you call me?"

Then Eli realized it was the Lord who was calling the boy. So he said to Samuel, "Go and lie down again, and if someone calls again, say, 'Speak, Lord, your servant is listening.'" So Samuel went back to bed.

And the Lord called as before, "Samuel! Samuel!"

And Samuel replied, "Speak, your servant is listening."

Then the Lord said to Samuel, "I am about to do a shocking thing in Israel…"

1 Samuel 3:1-11 (NLT)

This is just the beginning of the story of Samuel. God used Samuel in many powerful ways.

However, I was told to read about the calling of Samuel. What I read was very encouraging to me, because it showed that God spoke to Samuel and called him when he was a young boy and did not even know God.

That would have been enough for me to feel encouraged, but then God put a thought in my head that sent an electric bolt of excitement through my body. "Find out how old Samuel was, when I called him."

I immediately knew the point of that thought. I

had been 12 when God spoke to me. If the first thing I found out about how old Samuel had been when God first spoke to him indicated Samuel had been 12 at that time, I knew I would have received a great and powerful sign.

I looked in the Bible, but it did not say how old Samuel was when God first spoke to him. Then, I typed the question into the computer. It said that, according to the first-century Jewish historian Josephus, Samuel was 12 years old, when God first spoke to him! That was an electrifyingly powerful sign to me. I know there are disagreements among scholars about how old Samuel was when God first spoke to him, but the first answer I got was the sign I had been holding my breath hoping to receive.

That was more than enough encouragement for me. But, God wasn't through encouraging me that night. The next thought that came to me was, "What else do you and Samuel have in common?" I read the story of Samuel again, and I saw it. Samuel had been given up by his mother when he was a baby and, in a sense, adopted by Eli.

I had been adopted, too! I will never know why my biological mother gave me up, but she did. However, I do know that the most important thing on the minds of my Momma and Daddy, who adopted me, was to teach me about God. I remember one summer, before I knew how to read, when my mother spent every day making me memorize the catechism of the Presbyterian Church. I am not saying this because I think it is a great accomplishment. I am saying it because it shows how important God was to my Momma and Daddy, who adopted me and taught me to love God.

Maybe some people will read this and not be moved by it. Maybe some people will not think it is so important. Maybe some people will think everything I have written is a combination of imagination, wishful thinking, and coincidences. I cannot control what anybody else thinks. But, I hope somebody will read this and see what it means to me. God, the same God who created the universe, cares enough about regular people like me to notice when we are discouraged and to take his time to encourage us to keep on trying to do what He has called us to do. That is both amazing and encouraging to me.

Dear God, How can you do everything you have to do and still find the time to send messages to me about things in the Bible you want me to read? It is wonderful to know that the same voice that spoke the world into existence also speaks to regular people like me! In Jesus' name, Amen

MESSAGE 4

Nehemiah

The cycle of discouragement, to encouragement from God, to high hope, to failure, and then to more discouragement continued to repeat itself in my life. The more times this happened, the more depressed I got and the closer I came to giving up. I wondered if I had sinned and failed so much that I was not a fit person to take a message from God. I prayed so much that I got sick of praying. I began to feel like I had just made a fool out of myself again. Then, on another night while I was watching TV with my wife, I got another message from God. "Read about Nehemiah."

I didn't know anything about Nehemiah. All I knew to do was to start reading the book of Nehemiah and to try to figure out why God told me to read it.

Had Nehemiah been concerned about something that was not going well? Had he let depression overtake him? If so, what did he do about it?

Hanani, one of my brothers, came to visit me with some other men who had just arrived from Judah. I asked them about the Jews who had returned there from captivity and about how things were going in Jerusalem.

They said to me, "Things are not going well for those who returned to the province of Judah. They are in great trouble and disgrace. The wall of Jerusalem has been torn down, and the gates have been destroyed by fire."

When I heard this, I sat down and wept. In fact, for days I mourned, fasted, and prayed to the God of Heaven. Then I said,

"O Lord, God of Heaven, the great and awesome God who keeps his covenant of unfailing love with those who love Him and obey his commandments, listen to

my prayer! Look down and see me praying night and day for your people Israel. I confess that we have sinned against you. Yes, even my own family and I have sinned! We have sinned terribly by not obeying the commands, decrees, and regulations that you gave us through your servant Moses..."

Nehemiah 1:2-7 (NLT)

I noticed that things were going terribly for something that Nehemiah cared about very much. He had wept, mourned, fasted and prayed night and day to God for days without getting any results. I could identify with how he felt. He also wondered if his sins were the thing preventing God from turning the situation around. So, he then prayed a different prayer.

But, unlike the prayers he had been praying, this prayer was not about his goal. This prayer was about Nehemiah's own sin. In it, he confessed his sin. Only after confessing his sins did he end his prayer by asking for God's help.

"O Lord, please hear my prayer! Listen to the prayers of those of us who delight in honoring you. Please grant me success today by making the king favorable to me. Put it into his heart to be kind to me." In those days I was the king's cup-bearer.

Nehemiah 1:11 (NLT)

A cup-bearer was an officer of high rank in the king's court. His duty was to pour and serve drinks at the king's table. Since the king had a terrible fear of being poisoned, Nehemiah had to be considered totally trustworthy to be given that responsibility.

So, the steps Nehemiah followed were to confess his sins first and then to ask God to touch the king's heart to help him achieve his goal. Once he prayed that prayer, he was ready to use his position to ask the king to help him achieve his goal. I thought that would be a good formula to follow in my prayers.

However, even after this, nothing improved! Things kept getting worse! How could this be? Nehemiah was trying to do something that God wanted him to do. He had confessed his sins. He had asked God to touch the king's heart to be favorable to him. Yet, day after day, things only got worse and Nehemiah only got more depressed with each passing day. Scholars say this went on for four long, agonizing months. Then, when Nehemiah became so depressed that he no longer expected anything positive to happen, God used Nehemiah's depression to touch the king's heart.

Early in the following spring, in the month of Nisan, during the twentieth year of King Artaxerxes' reign, I was serving the king his wine. I had never before appeared sad in his presence. So the king asked me,

"Why are you looking so sad? You don't look sick to me. You must be deeply troubled."

Then I was terrified, but I replied, "Long live the king! How can I not be sad? For the city where my ancestors are buried is in ruins, and the gates have been destroyed by fire."

The king asked, "Well, how can I help you?"

With a prayer to the God of Heaven, I replied, "If it please the king, and if you are pleased with me, your servant, send me to Judah to rebuild the city where my ancestors are buried."

The king, with the queen sitting beside him, asked, "How long will you be gone? When will you return?" After I told him how long I would be gone, the king agreed to my request.

Nehemiah 2:1-6 (NLT)

This lifted my depression and gave me encouragement. Here, in the Bible, was the record of a great man, Nehemiah, who God had called to achieve an important goal for Him. But, Nehemiah saw no progress at all. Every day, the situation got bleaker and more depressing. Even when Nehemiah confessed his sins, things still seemed to be getting more and more hopeless. No matter how hard and long Nehemiah prayed, mourned and fasted, there was no progress.

As the days went by, Nehemiah got so depressed that he could no longer hide his sadness from the king. Nehemiah was at the point of giving up. But, just at Nehemiah's lowest point, God used Nehemiah's depression to get the king's attention. Then, God touched the king's heart and finally got Nehemiah the permission he needed to begin making progress on achieving his call from God to rebuild the temple wall.

This showed me that just because God was not

responding to my prayers to allow me to make progress towards achieving what He had called me to do, that did not mean that I had failed or misunderstood what God had told me. It just meant that I needed to have the faith to be patient and wait for God to touch people's hearts. God had not failed to help me. I had failed to trust God.

Dear God, Thank you for showing me that sometimes you use difficult things, even sickness or depression, to help people accomplish your goals for their lives. In Jesus' name, Amen

MESSAGE 5

Jeremiah

Despite all this encouragement I had received from God, it didn't take too many days of seeing absolutely no progress for me to get very discouraged again. Intellectually, I could understand the lessons that God was teaching me. But, that was just in my mind. In my heart and soul, the lessons God had taught me could not keep my depression from coming back.

I was making no progress towards the goal that God had called me to achieve. The more time that went by with nothing positive happening, the more depressed I got. If my testimony was ever going to reach people, it seemed like it should have already happened. I still thought that God would use *The*

Nine Words to help people one day, but I gave up on the hope that He would do this during my lifetime.

Then, on another night while I was sitting with my wife and watching TV again, I got another message. This one was, "Read about the discouragement of Jeremiah." As I had done in response to the other messages, I stopped what I was doing and started reading about Jeremiah.

The first thing I noticed was that Jeremiah was known as "The Weeping Prophet." Then, I read about his call.

The Lord gave me this message.

"I knew you before I formed you in your mother's womb. Before you were born I set you apart and appointed you as my prophet to the nations."

"O Sovereign Lord," I said, "I can't speak for you! I'm too young!"

The Lord replied, "Don't say, 'I'm too young,' for you

must go wherever I send you and say whatever I tell you. And don't be afraid of the people, for I will be with you and will protect you. I, the Lord, have spoken!"

Then the Lord reached out and touched my mouth and said,

"Look, I have put my words in your mouth! Today I appoint you to stand up against nations and kingdoms. Some you must uproot and tear down, destroy and overthrow. Others you must build up and plant."

Then the Lord said to me, "Look, Jeremiah! What do you see?"

And I replied, "I see a branch from an almond tree."

And the Lord said, "That's right, and it means that I am watching, and I will certainly carry out my plans."

Jeremiah 1:4–12 (NLT)

Wow! A lot in this caught my attention. God said that He knew Jeremiah even before he was formed in his mother's womb. That's amazing. But, it is also consistent with my thoughts. I believe that before my wife and I were formed in our mothers' wombs, God had already decided that we should marry each other. This scripture certainly supported that belief. And I don't think there is anything more special about Jeremiah, my wife, or me than there is about anybody else. I think God knows all people and has plans for them before they are formed in their mother's wombs. If anybody thinks I write the things I write because I think I am special, they are completely mistaken. I think everybody is equally special to God, and that He has plans for everybody.

This also shows that Jeremiah was very young when God first spoke to him and called him. Authorities think this happened between the time Jeremiah was a pre-teen and the time he reached 24 years of age. At any rate, Jeremiah was very young when God first spoke to him and called him, and Jeremiah had the same reaction that I had when God spoke to me. Jeremiah told God he couldn't do what God called him to do. And the reason he gave God for this was that he thought he was too young.

It seems to make God a little mad when people tell God that they can't do what God calls them to do. In my case, I just knew that I, a 12 year old boy, had no way to cause a popular and pretty girl to ever marry me, as God had told me I should do. I think the problem the people being called have with their calling is that they measure what God has called them to do against their ability to do it by themselves. I think they should measure what God has called them to do against God's ability to get it done, not their own ability.

I know that, in my case, I did everything that I could to achieve what God called me to do, and I failed so miserably that I finally gave up. But, the minute that I gave up on achieving the goal that God called me to achieve, God immediately stepped in and made it happen. So, I believe that when God calls people to do something, they should not ask themselves if they can do it, because they never can. They should ask themselves if God can do it, because God always can!

The last thing in this scripture that made an impression on me was that God told Jeremiah that He would be watching Jeremiah, and that He would definitely carry out the plans He had for Jeremiah. When God called me to marry my wife, I suffered through many painful ups and downs during the following eight years. Sometimes, it felt like God was doing nothing to help me achieve what He called me to do. But, not seeing what God is doing to make His plan for our lives work out does not mean that God is not doing things every day to make what He called us to do come to pass.

So, you would have thought that with a beginning like that, Jeremiah's story would be fulfilled quickly and happily. But, that is the opposite of what really happened. Jeremiah tried to get people to listen to the message that God had given him for forty years in a row, and nobody would listen to him. Finally, Jeremiah got so depressed and exhausted that He accused God of playing with him or tricking him.

O Lord, you misled me, and I allowed myself to be misled. You are stronger than I am, and you overpowered me. Now I am mocked every day; everyone laughs at me. When I speak, the words burst out. "Violence and destruction!" I shout. So these messages from the Lord have made me a household joke. But if I say I'll never mention the Lord or speak in His name, His word burns in my heart like a fire. It's like a fire in my bones! I am worn out trying to hold it in! I can't do it!

Jeremiah 20:7-9 (NLT)

Later on, the scriptures show that Jeremiah expressed even more depression and frustration.

Yet I curse the day I was born! May no one celebrate the day of my birth. I curse the messenger who told my father, "Good news—you have a son!" Let him be destroyed like the cities of old that the Lord overthrew without mercy. Terrify him all day long with battle shouts, because he did not kill me at birth. Oh, that I had died in my mother's womb, that her body had been my grave! Why was I ever born? My entire life has been filled with trouble, sorrow and shame.

Jeremiah 20:14-18 (NLT)

Well, I can heartily identify with most of the feelings Jeremiah expressed. I have had anxiety and depression all my life. But, wow! That man was even more depressed than I ever got. I used to be a criminal defense attorney. If I ever met with a client who told me the things that Jeremiah said, I would have immediately filed a plea of "Not Guilty by Reason of Mental Defect or Disease."

Nonetheless, some things cannot be denied. Jeremiah did write these things, and he was following through on God's calling to him. But, was he forgotten and thrown on the dustbin of history? Absolutely not. He is today an important figure in both Judaism and Christianity, is quoted in The New Testament, and is regarded as a prophet by Islam. When he was in the throes of his deep depression, Jeremiah probably would have never believed that approximately 2,500 years after he wrote these words, they would be in an honored book in practically every home on a continent that he never even knew existed.

Reading about what Jeremiah went through trying to carry out his calling from God encouraged me. By showing me that Jeremiah was able to fulfill his calling from God, in spite of the fact that he felt just as lost and depressed as I do, God definitely encouraged me not to give up.

Dear God, Help me to understand that being called by you does not mean there is smooth sailing ahead. Like being drafted into the Army, it is not an invitation to a party. It is an opportunity to serve. In Jesus' name, Amen

MESSAGE 6

God Helps those He Calls

During the Christmas season of 2021, I knew that I would not be able to continue the work I had been doing as a lawyer. I had been diagnosed with Parkinsonism about seven years earlier. The symptoms had gotten to the point that they prevented me from going to Court four or five days a week, as I had been doing for many years.

I prayed and asked God to show me what I could do to make the money we needed every month during 2022. To my surprise, God responded to my prayer by telling me that I should write a book about the nine words he spoke to me when I was 12 years old and the miracles He had done in the ensuing eight years to make what He told me to do come to pass.

That didn't seem like a very practical idea to me. I told God that it would be hard for me to write a book, when I didn't know if we were going to be able to pay our rent and our other necessary bills that were due in a few weeks. I told God that I would try to write the book, if He would help get us the money we needed to keep going.

I wrote five people I thought God had put it on my heart to write and ask for financial help. I explained to them what God had told me to do and that I could not do it without the financial help for which I was asking. These were very good, Christian people. But, I didn't hear anything back from them.

One day, I knew that we would not be able to stay in our home or pay for our necessities unless I got some financial help right away. As I walked out to our mail box, I prayed. I said, "God, I don't care what happens to me. I don't care if I live or die. But, please take care of my family." When I opened our mail box, I saw two envelopes. One was from a girl I had gone to high school with and had not seen since 1968. The other was from a former basketball coach at Georgia Tech, my favorite team.

I had written both of them asking for their help, but had given up on hearing back from them. But, when I opened those envelopes, they both had checks in them. The checks totaled $1,650, the amount that we needed to pay our bills for the coming month. I was overcome with emotion. I went back into our house and handed the checks to my wife. I couldn't even speak.

My wife looked at them. She knew we had received a very big miracle. She looked at me and said, "Are you going to write that book now? You told God you would, if He provided the money we needed to live."

That night, after she went to bed, I stayed up and

started writing the story. I did that every night for several weeks. It was not hard to do, since I was just describing what had happened to me.

But, when I finished the short, little book, I did not know what to do next. I asked God what I should do, and I got the answer that I should send the draft of my book to some people I knew. I sent it to about ten people. I didn't hear back from most of them, and most of the ones who did reply told me they didn't like the book. I got very discouraged again. I thought, "What is the point of this?"

Then one day, from out of nowhere, I got a message from a girl I went to high school with but had not seen since 1966. She wrote, "I want to help you get your book published." If God had not called her to do that, I can't imagine how the book could have ever made it past my computer screen. But, with God's help, she got it published.

I looked in the Bible to see if other people God called to do things needed God to call special people to help them. It turns out that they did. Here are some examples.

But Moses pleaded with the Lord, "O Lord, I'm not very good with words. I never have been, and I'm not now, even though you have spoken to me. I get tonguetied, and my words get tangled."

Then the Lord asked Moses, "Who makes a person's mouth? Who decides whether people speak or do not speak, hear or do not hear, see or do not see? Is it not I, the Lord? Now go! I will be with you as you speak, and I will instruct you in what to say."

But Moses again pleaded, "Lord, please! Send anyone else."

Then the Lord became angry with Moses. "All right," *He said. "What about your brother, Aaron the Levite? I know he speaks well. And look! He is on his way to meet you now. He will be delighted to see you. Talk to him,*

and put the words in his mouth. I will be with both of

you as you speak, and I will instruct you both in what

to do. Aaron will be your spokesman to the people. He

will be your mouthpiece, and you will stand in the place

of God for him, telling him what to say."

Exodus 4:10-16 (NLT)

So, God helped Moses by calling Aaron to help him.

Then, there was Elijah. After witnessing and being a part of many miracles, Elijah got so terribly discouraged that he fled as far away as he could get, collapsed, and told God that he had enough and wanted to die. Then, God sent someone to help Elijah, too.

Then he lay down and slept under the broom tree. But as he was sleeping, an angel touched him and told him, "Get up and eat!" He looked around and there beside his head was some bread baked on hot stones and a jar of water! So he ate and drank and lay down again.

Then the angel of the Lord came again and touched him and said, "Get up and eat some more, or the journey ahead will be too much for you."

So he got up and ate and drank, and the food gave him enough strength to travel forty days and forty nights to Mount Sinai, the mountain of God. There he came to a cave, where he spent the night.

But the Lord said to him, "What are you doing here, Elijah?"

Elijah replied, "I have zealously served the Lord God Almighty. But the people of Israel have broken their covenant with you, torn down your altars, and killed every one of your prophets. I am the only one left, and now they are trying to kill me, too."

1 Kings 19:5-10 (NLT)

Seeing the distress that he was in, God told Elijah to go and anoint Elisha to replace him as God's prophet. Just as God had told Moses to get Aaron to help him accomplish his calling, God told Elijah to get Elisha to help him accomplish his calling.

Then, there is the story of Jeremiah and Baruch. It is particularly exciting to me, because it involves Jeremiah being told by God to write an account of the messages that God had given to him, like God told me to write a book about the words He had spoken to me and the miracles He did to make them come to pass. But, Jeremiah and I had the same problem. We could not get the message that God had told us to write out to the people that God wanted it to reach. So, we both needed God to call a special person to help us do something that we could not do.

In Jeremiah's case, the person God called to help him was Baruch. Jeremiah told Baruch the messages that God had given him, and Baruch wrote them down and took them to the King, the person God wanted Jeremiah's message to reach. In the same way, God touched the heart of a wonderful person to help me. Without her help, I don't know how *The Nine Words* would have ever gotten published.

The lesson I got from these stories is very comforting to me. When God calls a person to do something for Him, He will touch the hearts of special people to help the person He has called.

Dear God, Thank you for sending special people to help us do what you call us to do. In Jesus' name, Amen

Message 7

Jonah

Up until now, I have not received any more messages from God to read about specific people in the Bible who were called by God but got deeply discouraged and depressed. However, the stories of the people that I did get messages to read about made me interested in looking at other people in the Bible to learn about their calling and to see if they got discouraged.

One that came to my mind was Jonah. My Daddy died in 1973, but I have never forgotten what a wonderful man he was. He was an Elder and adult Sunday School teacher at every church we belonged to while I was growing up. When he died, I got the last Bible he ever had. When I looked through it, I found one sheet of paper on which Daddy had made some notes for a Sunday School class he taught on Jonah. This is what he wrote:

"9/10/72

"Jonah

"Chapter I

"1. Most Impt. Idea

"2. Purpose. How God works through and with people

"Written about 8th century BC.

"Written by Jonah.

"1. Word to Jonah

"2. Jonah's God the working God

"3. Conversion of Crew.

"Procrastination

"This was written at a later date & because of this it had to be in the past tense."

Well, those are my Daddy's notes, exactly as he wrote them back in 1972. I still have the original. It means a lot to me to see that back in 1972 my Daddy was considering the same thing that I am dwelling on all these years later, "How God works through and with people."

The calling of Jonah is described in the Bible as follows:

The Lord gave this message to Jonah son of Amittai: "Get up and go to the great city of Nineveh. Announce my judgment against it because I have seen how wicked its people are."

But Jonah got up and went in the opposite direction to get away from the Lord. He went down to the port of Joppa, where he found a ship leaving for Tarshish. He bought a ticket and went on board, hoping to escape from the Lord by sailing to Tarshish."

Jonah 1:1-3 (NLT)

Well, a lot of people that God has called to do something for Him have tried to convince God that they weren't the right person for the job. But, Jonah is the first person I have read about who actually thought that he could hide from God! As you would suspect, Jonah was not able to hide from God. God watched every step that Jonah took. While Jonah was at sea on board that ship, God caused a great storm to come up. Jonah knew everybody on the ship was in trouble because he had tried to hide from God. When the other people on the ship confronted Jonah about what he had done, Jonah was very distraught.

"Throw me into the sea," Jonah said, "and it will become calm again. I know that this terrible storm is all my fault."

Jonah 1:12 (NLT)

The sailors threw Jonah into the sea, and the storm stopped.

Now the Lord had arranged for a great fish to swallow Jonah. And Jonah was inside the fish for three days and three nights.

Jonah 1:17 (NLT)

You might think this was the low point for Jonah, but that would be incorrect. In the belly of the great fish, Jonah prayed to God, repented, and asked for mercy. God then caused the fish to spit up Jonah. After that, Jonah went to do what God had called him to do. He went to Nineveh and told the people to repent. They did, and God changed his mind and did not destroy them. This would seem like a successful mission accomplished, but that wasn't how Jonah felt about it. He was mad that God had changed his mind and spared the people of Nineveh. Incredibly, that was Jonah's low point.

The change of plans greatly upset Jonah, and he became very angry. So he complained to the Lord about it: "Didn't I say before I left home that you would do this, Lord? That is why I ran away to Tarshish! I knew that you are a merciful and compassionate God, slow to get angry and filled with unfailing love. You are eager to turn back from destroying people. Just kill me now, Lord! I'd rather be dead than alive if what I predicted will not happen."

The Lord replied, "Is it right for you to be angry about this?"

Then Jonah went out to the east side of the city and made a shelter to sit under as he waited to see what would happen to the city. And the Lord God arranged for a leafy plant to grow there and soon it spread its broad leaves over Jonah's head, shading him from the sun. This eased his discomfort, and Jonah was very grateful for the plant.

But God also arranged for a worm! The next morning at dawn the worm ate through the plant so that it withered away. And as the sun grew hot, God arranged for a scorching east wind to blow on Jonah. The sun beat down on his head until he grew faint and wished to die. "Death is certainly better than living like this!" he exclaimed.

Then God said to Jonah, "Is it right for you to be angry because the plant died?"

"Yes," Jonah retorted, "even angry enough to die!"

Then the Lord said, "You feel sorry about the plant, though you did nothing to put it there. It came quickly and died quickly. But Nineveh has more than 120,000 people living in spiritual darkness, not to mention all the animals. Shouldn't I feel sorry for such a great city?"

Jonah 4:1-11 (NLT)

There are a lot of lessons to learn from this story. When Jonah was in the fish, he repented and wanted God to be merciful to him. But, when the people of Nineveh repented because of the message Jonah brought to them from God, Jonah did not want God to be merciful to them. If we want mercy for ourselves, we must also want mercy for other people, too.

And any time we get upset because God's decision is different from what we want to see happen, we should hear God asking us the same question that God asked Jonah. Is it really right for us to be angry?

So, during the time that Jonah was trying to answer God's call to him, Jonah got so depressed that he wanted to die. Well, that is encouraging to me, because it is another example of a person in the Bible that God called to do a specific task who got very discouraged. If these Biblical prophets got such deep depression and discouragement, I should not feel like

I have wandered off the beaten path when I feel that way, too. After all, God eventually made their answer to His call successful. So, maybe He will make my calling from Him come to pass, too.

Dear God, Help me to always show the same mercy to other people that you have always shown to me. In Jesus' name, Amen

MESSAGE 8

Why I wasn't Forgiven

"If you forgive those who sin against you, your Heavenly Father will forgive you."

Matthew 6:14 (NLT)

I have read this verse many times. I always thought that I had forgiven everybody, yet I never felt forgiven. I wrote this off to some sort of humility. I thought that I had forgiven everybody else and that God had forgiven me. But, I thought that it wouldn't seem like I really cared about my sins, if I forgave myself. So, I didn't.

It wasn't until I was working on this devotional that I saw that I had completely missed the point. The lack of forgiveness I was feeling was not because I had not forgiven myself. The lack of forgiveness I was feeling was because God had not forgiven me!

Wow! That is a blow. Here I was, sure that I had forgiven everybody and that God had forgiven me. But, I was wrong. I had not forgiven everybody, because I had not forgiven myself. And because of that, God had not forgiven me! That's why I didn't feel forgiven. I wasn't forgiven!

But, how could that be? I never thought of it before, but now it crystal clear.

That scripture says, "If you forgive those who sin against you, your Heavenly Father will forgive you." So, where did I go wrong?

The key to me understanding my problem was to honestly answer this question: Who has sinned against me more than anybody else? The answer is "me." I have sinned against myself much more than everybody else combined has sinned against me. Every time I sinned against God or another person, I sinned against myself more. My sins against other people were horrible, but my sins' worst consequences were on me, not on the other people that I sinned against.

For instance, if I lied to somebody, they suffered negative consequences. But, they didn't lose their self-respect. But, I did.

If I stole money from somebody, they suffered the serious consequences of losing their money. But, they didn't lose their self-respect. But, I did.

If I cheated somebody, they felt hurt and loss. But, they didn't lose their self-respect. But, I did.

Every time I committed one of my many thousands of sins, the people I sinned against lost something of great value. But, they didn't lose their self-respect. But, I did.

After a lifetime of sinning, I had no self-respect left. That's the very opposite of what Jesus died on the cross for. He didn't give up his life on the cross so that I could have absolutely no self-respect.

"The thief's purpose is to steal and kill and destroy. My purpose is to give them a rich and satisfying life."

John 10:10 (NLT)

Whose purpose was I accomplishing by refusing to forgive myself and ending up with no self-respect? The Devil's! I was doing exactly what the Devil wanted me to do! By refusing to forgive myself, as I would have happily and quickly forgiven anyone else, I let the Devil steal my-self-respect, kill my joy, and destroy my peace of mind.

The very worst thing was that by refusing to forgive myself, I was making it absolutely impossible for God to forgive me. I was not doing what God wanted me to do. God wanted me to forgive myself, have self-respect, and have a rich and satisfying life.

In refusing to forgive myself, I was disobeying God's requirement for Him to forgive me. Jesus said that I must forgive those who sin against me in order for Him to forgive me! But, I was refusing to forgive the person who sinned against me the most. Me! That may not seem like a big revelation to anybody else, but it is probably the biggest revelation that I have ever received.

That brings up the next question. How many times should I forgive myself? Once, twice, three times?

Then Peter came to Him and asked, "Lord, how often should I forgive someone who sins against me? Seven times?"

"No, not seven times," Jesus replied, "but seventy times seven!"

Matthew 18:21-22 (NLT)

The inescapable conclusion from this is that I am commanded by Jesus to forgive everyone who sins against me, including myself. I must forgive all the people—including myself—who sin against me every time they sin against me, no matter how many times that is!

Dear God, Help me to remember that, in order to be forgiven by you, I must first forgive myself. In Jesus' name, Amen

MESSAGE 9

Your Time and Your Choice

There is a popular perception that the minute you are born, you start to die. That every day you wake up, you are closer to the end. That life is a game that everybody loses.

My wife and I got married in 1970. In 1972, I got drafted. I hated being away from her at Basic Training. I got very depressed. Thank God, she wrote me a lot of letters. I remember one in which she said words to the effect that, "This will all be over soon, and we will be back together. Time is on our side."

Well, now we have been married over 53 years. Sometimes, I get depressed because I do not feel like time is on our side anymore. But, that is exactly how the Devil wants us to feel. Time is the Devil's secret weapon. He uses it to manufacture depression.

But, the Devil is a liar. Time is on our side. We are not approaching death. We are approaching Heaven. Jesus promised us that was the case. If we don't believe that, we believe that Jesus is a liar. But, Jesus is not a liar. It's the Devil who's the liar.

But tell me this—since we preach that Christ rose from the dead, why are some of you saying there will be no resurrection of the dead? For, if there is no resurrection of the dead, then Christ has not been raised either. And if Christ has not been raised, then all our preaching is useless, and your faith is useless.

1 Corinthians 15:12-14 (NLT)

And if our hope in Christ is only for this life, we are more to be pitied than anyone in the world.

1 Corinthians 15:19 (NLT)

Then, when our dying bodies have been transformed into bodies that will never die, this scripture will be fulfilled:

"Death is swallowed up in victory. O death, where is your victory? O death, where is your sting?"

1 Corinthians 15:54-55 (NLT)

I have not written one thing in these pages that the human nature of man cannot find an easy reason to ridicule and dismiss. The stories in The Old Testament are ancient and seem to some like fairy tales. The philosophy of The New Testament is a little less old, but seems to some like wishful thinking.

Many will say that nothing in the Bible can be proven.

The people who believe that will put their faith in the smartest doctors, scientists and philosophers. They will trust the intelligence of people to keep them going as long as possible and then, in an act they consider the pinnacle of reason and courage, they will choose to die without seeking comfort from the thing they look down on as religious superstition. In short, these people will die with pride that they were brave enough to not even ask God to save them. They will think they are wise, but they will be making the most foolish mistake of all.

Only fools say in their hearts, "There is no God." They are corrupt, and their actions are evil; not one of them does good!

Psalm 14:1 (NLT)

As for the people who say there is no proof of God or anything about Him, let me tell them this. He talked to me when I was 12 years old. He talked to me because He cared about who I should marry. After that, He performed many miracles to get my wife and me married. Since He got us married, He has continued to do countless miracles to keep us together. So, God does exist. He is personal, powerful and accessible. He loves regular people like my wife and me, and He intervenes often in our lives!

God loves atheists just as much as He loves believers. He wants to have a relationship with everybody. He is ready to hear from everybody right now. But, if people are too intellectual or too proud to hear Him calling, there is nothing God can do to help them.

Remember what it says: "Today when you hear His voice, don't harden your hearts as Israel did when they rebelled."

Hebrews 3:15 (NLT)

While I was typing this very last paragraph, I was sitting at my computer in the middle of the night. I was the only person awake in my house. I heard something strange in the next room. I got scared. I thought it was either a thief or Jesus coming to get me. I was so horrified that I got up out of my chair and went looking for what I had heard.

I realized that I was scared to see Jesus face to face. I realized that I wasn't near ready to see Him. But, I better get used to it, because soon He will be coming to get me. Soon, He will be coming to get everybody.

Feeling close enough to God to be scared that Jesus is in the next room is an incredibly encouraging thing. It means I believe. I might be scared, but I do believe!

For you know quite well that the day of the Lord's return will come unexpectedly, like a thief in the night.

1 Thessalonians 5:2 (NLT)

Dear God, Thank you for showing me that I really do believe in you. In Jesus' name, Amen

MESSAGE 10

A Thorn in Our Flesh?

There is a very popular question that has been asked very often. Books have been written about it. This question is, "Why do bad things happen to good people?" It is almost impossible for people not to ask this question and not try to come up with an answer for it.

If I wanted to boast, I would be no fool in doing so, because I would be telling the truth. But I won't do it, because I don't want anyone to give me credit beyond what they can see in my life or hear in my message, even though I have received such wonderful revelations from God. So to keep me from becoming proud, I was given a thorn in my flesh, a messenger from Satan to torment me and keep me from becoming proud.

Three different times I begged the Lord to take it away. Each time He said, "My grace is all you need. My power works best in weakness." So now I am glad to boast about my weaknesses, so that the power of Christ can work through me.

2 Corinthians 12:6-9 (NLT)

In this scripture, Paul clearly presents himself as a good person. Then, he describes a pain he has that God will not take away. So, right there, Paul has asked this same age-old and very popular question, "Why do bad things happen to good people?" Then, as smart people cannot resist doing, Paul comes up with an answer that at least satisfies him. He believes that he has a pain that God will not take away because it is making him a better person.

You will notice that in the question, "Why do bad things happen to good people?", the good people are absolved from responsibility for the bad things that happen to them. That is why it is such a popular question.

There is another question that is not nearly as popular. I don't know of any books that have been written about it. That question is, "Why do good people do bad things?" That question makes us feel uncomfortable, not reassured. This is because that question puts the responsibility for many bad things on good people.

Many people have speculated about exactly what Paul's pain was. I have always thought Paul's pain was his horrible guilt over the Christians he martyred and persecuted when he went by the name of Saul. No matter how much good he did as Paul, I believe that Paul could not close his eyes to go to sleep at night without seeing the face of Stephen being stoned to death and the faces of the many other Christians he persecuted. After all, you can change your name, but you can't change your past.

"You stubborn people! You are heathen at heart and deaf to the truth. Must you forever resist the Holy Spirit? That's what your ancestors did, and so do you! Name one prophet your ancestors didn't persecute! They even killed the ones who predicted the coming of the Righteous One—the Messiah whom you betrayed and murdered. You deliberately disobeyed God's law, even though you received it from the hands of angels."

The Jewish leaders were infuriated by Stephen's accusation, and they shook their fists at him in rage. But Stephen, full of the Holy Spirit, gazed steadily into Heaven and saw the glory of God, and he saw Jesus standing in the place of honor at God's right hand. And he told them, "Look, I see the heavens opened and the Son of Man standing in the place of honor at God's right hand!"

Then they put their hands over their ears and began shouting. They rushed at him and dragged him out of the city and began to stone him. His accusers took off their coats and laid them at the feet of a young man named Saul.

As they stoned him, Stephen prayed, "Lord Jesus, receive my spirit." He fell to his knees, shouting, "Lord, don't charge them with this sin." And with that, he died.

Saul was one of the witnesses and he agreed completely with the killing of Stephen.

A great wave of persecution began that day, sweeping over the church in Jerusalem; and all the believers except the apostles were scattered through the regions of Judea and Samaria. (Some devout men came and buried Stephen with great mourning.) But Saul was going everywhere to destroy the church. He went from house to house, dragging out both men and women to throw them into prison.

Acts 7:51-60 and Acts 8:1-3 (NLT)

Meanwhile, Saul was uttering threats with every breath and was eager to kill the Lord's followers. So he went to the high priest. He requested letters addressed to the synagogues in Damascus, asking for their cooperation in the arrest of any followers of the Way he found there. He wanted to bring them—both men and women—back to Jerusalem in chains.

As he was approaching Damascus on this mission, a light from Heaven suddenly shone down around him. He fell to the ground and heard a voice saying to him, "Saul! Saul! Why are you persecuting me?"

"Who are you, lord?" Saul asked.

And the voice replied, "I am Jesus, the one you are persecuting! Now get up and go into the city, and you will be told what you must do."

The men with Paul stood speechless, for they heard the sound of someone's voice but saw no one! Saul picked himself up off the ground, but when he opened his eyes *he was blind. So his companions led him by the hand to Damascus. He remained there blind for three days and did not eat or drink.*

Now there was a believer in Damascus named Ananias. The Lord spoke to him in a vision, calling, "Ananias!"

"Yes, Lord!" he replied.

Then the Lord said, "Go over to Straight Street, to the house of Judas. When you get there, ask for a man from Tarsus named Saul. He is praying to me right now. I have shown him a vision of a man named Ananias coming in and laying hands on him so he can see again."

"But Lord," exclaimed Ananias, "I've heard many people talk about the terrible things this man has done to believers in Jerusalem! And he is authorized by the leading priests to arrest everyone who calls upon your name."

But the Lord said, "Go, for Saul is my chosen

instrument to take my message to the Gentiles and to

kings, as well as to the people of Israel. And I will show

him how much he must suffer for my name's sake."

I believe that the thorn that Paul thought was in his flesh was really in his heart. I believe that when God answered Paul's three requests for relief from this pain by saying that God's grace was all Paul needed and that God's power works best in weakness, God was explaining to Paul that the agony he felt over the way he had persecuted Christians was the reason that God chose him to be God's messenger.

Every person on earth should find the same wonderful encouragement in this true story from the Bible that I do. So, I thought that my sins and failures made me unfit to speak for God! Well, I committed a lot of terrible sins and hurt many good people, but I didn't witness and agree with the stoning of Billy Graham! I didn't grab Christians from out of their homes and persecute them because they believed in Jesus!

So, by showing me this story of Paul, God has shown me that he used a man who was every bit as much of a sinner as I am to write one-third of The New Testament! I believe that God is telling me, "Steve Dugan, get up and get going. I have a use for you to speak for me. Never think again that you have sinned too much to serve me. I have shown you the reason I like to use people just as flawed as you are!" What could be more encouraging than that?

Dear God, Thank you for being willing to use sinners like Paul and me. In Jesus' name, Amen

MESSAGE 11

Anxiety and Depression

Don't worry about anything; instead, pray about
everything. Tell God what you need, and thank Him for
all He has done. Then you will experience God's peace,
which exceeds anything we can understand. His peace
will guard your hearts and minds as you live in Christ
Jesus.

Philippians 4:6-7 (NLT)

That sounds good, but I haven't been able to do it. I
try to be honest in these messages. So, I need to tell you
that I have had depression and anxiety for as long as I
can remember. It is a bad thing to have. Considering
how many miracles God has performed for me, I feel
like in my case that it is similar to a sin, because it

shows my unwillingness to let go of my life completely and trust everything and everybody in it to God. But, if I said that I didn't worry all the time, I would just be committing another sin. I would be lying.

I have been to psychiatrists and psychologists about this. But, there is no line of reasoning that can convince me not to be afraid of life. Life is a scary thing. In my opinion, anybody who thinks they have their life under control is in a severe state of denial.

Now, I believe God has things under control. But, that doesn't always comfort me. Sometimes, it scares me. I know there is going to be a time when God thinks it is time for my wife or me to get very ill or just die suddenly. The Bible promises us that will happen. It could happen at any time. That really scares me. I am actually much less scared of the things people may do to me than I am of the things that God has promised to do to me.

I know that I shouldn't be afraid of what God is going to do. I should trust Him so much that I will gladly accept anything that He decides to do. But, I can't get comfortable with the uncertainty of life. Life horrifies me. This doesn't keep me from being happy. But, even during the best times of my life, the uncertainty of life is always on my mind. Nobody can talk me out of believing it for one simple reason. I know that it is undisputedly true.

Doctors can give me medicine that is powerful enough to make me quit thinking about the truth I fear. But, to be powerful enough to do that, the medicine also would be powerful enough to keep me from thinking about anything at all. That is no way to live. So, I don't take the medicine, and I don't spend time talking with people who are trying to convince me why I shouldn't worry about. I do pray a lot that

God will spare me from the inevitable things I fear so much for as long as possible.

But, my question for this devotional is whether having so much anxiety and depression makes me unfit to write a book about faith or messages about God for people to read. Might I actually do more harm than good?

David wrote the famous 23rd Psalm. It is so comforting that many people know the beautiful King James Version of it by heart.

The Lord is my shepherd; I shall not want.

He maketh me to lie down in green pastures: He leadeth me beside the still waters.

He restoreth my soul: He leadeth me in the paths of righteousness for his name's sake.

Yea, though I walk through the valley of the shadow of death, I will fear no evil: for Thou art with me; thy rod and thy staff they comfort me.

Thou preparest a table before me in the presence of mine enemies: Thou anointest my head with oil; my cup runneth over.

Surely goodness and mercy shall follow me all the days of my life: and I will dwell in the house of the Lord forever.

Psalm 23:1-6 (KJV)

When I read that, I think, "David had it all together. He was surely a good person to talk to people about God. Maybe I shouldn't even try to. After all, who could benefit from anything I say, when they already have the towering strength of David to turn to right in their own Bibles?"

But this same person, David, also wrote the following.

I cry out to the Lord; I plead for the Lord's mercy.

I pour out my complaints before Him and tell Him all my troubles. When I am overwhelmed, you alone know the way I should turn.

Wherever I go, my enemies have set traps for me.

I look for someone to come and help me, but no one gives me a passing thought!

No one will help me; no one cares a bit what happens to me.

Then I pray to you, O Lord. I say, "You are my place of refuge. You are all I really want in life.

Hear my cry, for I am very low.

Rescue me from my persecutors, for they are too strong for me.

Bring me out of prison so I can thank you. The godly will crowd around me, for you are good to me."

Psalm 142:1-7 (NLT)

Does that sound consistent with the 23rd Psalm? Not really. But, did those feelings make David unfit to serve God and to write and speak for Him?

"But God removed Saul and replaced him with David, a man about whom God said, 'I have found David son of Jesse, a man after my own heart. He will do everything I want him to do.'"

Acts 13:22 (NLT)

The person who expresses my feelings of anxiety and depression the best is Jesus, Himself. He was God and man, and yet He suffered the strongest anxiety and depression of anyone.

Jesus suffered great anxiety in the Garden of Gethsemane.

He took Peter and Zebedee's two sons, James and John, and He became anguished and distressed. He told them, "My soul is crushed with grief to the point of death. Stay here and keep watch with me."

He went on a little farther and bowed with his face to the ground, praying, "My Father! If it is possible, let this cup of suffering be taken away from me. Yet I want your will to be done, not mine."

Matthew 26:37-39 (NLT)

There he was, my Lord and Savior, feeling exactly what I, in my massive weakness, feel! Jesus asked God to alter his plans and to spare Him the pain of being crucified, if it could be done consistent with God's will. Jesus suffered the ultimate depression on the cross.

At about three o'clock, Jesus called out with a loud voice, "Eli, Eli, lema sabachthani?" which means "My God, my God, why have you abandoned me?"

Some of the bystanders misunderstood and thought he was calling for the prophet Elijah. One of them ran and filled a sponge with sour wine, holding it up to Him on a red stick so He could drink. But the rest said, "Wait! Let's see whether Elijah comes to save Him."

Then Jesus shouted out again, and He released his spirit. At that moment the curtain in the sanctuary of the Temple was torn in two, from top to bottom. The earth shook, rocks split apart, and tombs opened. The bodies of many godly men and women who had died were raised from the dead. They left the cemetery after Jesus' resurrection, went into the holy city of Jerusalem, and appeared to many people.

The Roman officer and the other soldiers at the crucifixion were terrified by the earthquake and all that had happened. They said, "This man truly was the Son of God!"

Matthew 27:46-54 (NLT)

I spend my entire life with a feeling of anxiety similar to what Jesus suffered in the Garden of Gethsemane. However, and this is an amazing revelation to me, I have never been as depressed as Jesus was on that cross! Never! When things have gone against what I begged God for, I have felt like I have failed God. But, I never felt like God had abandoned me.

So, how has this devotional encouraged me? It has answered my question about whether my anxiety and depression make me unfit to serve God and even write and speak for Him. David felt it, too. And, most gloriously reassuring to me, Jesus felt what I feel and more. Nobody should think that their anxiety and depression make them unfit to serve God and even write and speak for Him.

I noticed something else. It was after witnessing Jesus' agony and depression that the Roman soldiers were converted and said, "This man truly was the Son of God!"

We must never think that our weaknesses, no matter what they are, make us unqualified to serve God. Not only do they not make us unqualified, God may even use them to make us more qualified to serve Him than we would be without them.

Dear God, Thank You for showing me in the examples of David, who you said was a man after your own heart, and of Jesus, your own Son, that I am not unfit to serve you because of my depression and anxiety. Please use my weaknesses to help somebody. In Jesus' name, Amen

MESSAGE 12

Prayer

My prayers are too often a list of things I run through. I tend to pray for these things in this order:

(1) That my family and I can become closer to God (I figure God will like that and be impressed that I put Him at the top of my prayer list.)

(2) That my family can be closer to each other (I figure that is a good and sort of unselfish request that God will like, too.)

(3) That my family can have good health (Now, I am getting to the real reason for my prayer: my fears and my selfish desires.)

(4)   That my family will be provided for financially (More fears and selfish desires.)

(5)   That the work that I and the other people in my family are trying to do will achieve what God wants it to achieve (A sort of humble sounding way of saying, "Please help me be successful at something. If I could just make enough money, that would be one less thing I would have to worry about and pray about.")

(6)   That people outside my family will have specific problems in their lives resolved in a positive way (Well, you know, I ask people to pray for me, and I tell them I will pray for them, so here it is, and God might think it's unselfish and sort of noble. It might cause Him to look more favorably on the stuff I'm really much more worried about.)

(7) That God will bless everybody I know and everybody I don't know (Well, it sounds good and doesn't take but a few seconds.)

(8) That I repent for my sins and ask God to forgive me for them. (I really am sorry for my sins. But, I must think they're pretty good, or I would actually quit doing them and not have to seem sincere when I repent for the same things day after day after day. I hope God gives me credit for at least knowing what I'm doing is bad.)

(9) That God will know how much I appreciate all the wonderful things He has done for me and my family. (Well, the Bible says to include thanking God for everything He's done for me in all my prayers, so why wouldn't I do that?)

Those are my main concerns. I pray for these things all the time. I feel that I need to pray for them all almost every time I pray, so that God won't think I take anything for granted and possibly not look favorably on my prior requests in any of the areas I don't mention in my present prayer.

This is a burdensome prayer life. I don't enjoy praying this way, and I am pretty sure that God does not enjoy listening to these prayers, either. I have my ritualistic list of things that I want from God, and I pray like I don't trust Him to remember them from the last time I prayed for them. It's like He's sitting there waiting for me to leave something out so He can zap me.

This style of praying is the adult version of children praying the same thing night after night. "Now I lay me down to sleep, I pray the Lord my soul to keep. And if I die before I wake, I pray the Lord my soul to take."

I'm pretty sure this is not a good way for an adult to pray. But, since I have received a lot of what I wanted when I prayed this way, I am afraid to change. That's pitiful, but it's the truth.

I think God wants me to ask Him what his will is for me is in my prayers. But, I don't do that. I spend my prayer time mainly telling God what my will is and asking Him to make that happen.

I'm afraid my prayers are an attempted manipulation of God, not an exercise of submission to God. I'm afraid my prayers are self-centered, not God-centered. My prayers may be almost an act of superstition. I know they are the result of nervousness, fear and desperation.

I am a Protestant, but I have come to admire the Catholic policy of not allowing priests to be married. If you have a family that you love, it is practically impossible not to make your prayers about your family, instead of about God. I suppose I think that God can take real good care of Himself, so I don't need to pray for Him. It's my family that's in jeopardy, and I want to spend my time in prayer focusing on my family. To be honest, I want God to focus on taking care of my family, too. This is because I am very scared of bad things happening to my family. The only defense I see to this is for God to miraculously protect the members of my family and provide for all their needs.

When I was a lawyer and had a jury trial, I did everything I could to speak effectively to the jury. I would never have conducted a trial by telling the jury, "Please let my client off. He will do better if you just give him another chance," over and over and over again. The reason I would not have done that is because the jury would not have liked it. It would not have kept their attention, and it would not have helped my client. But, the jury was composed of twelve people. I could look at them. I took the jury seriously, because they were right there. I never had to wonder if the jury existed. I never had any doubt that the jury existed. I respected the jury, because the jury had some power over my client's life.

I'm horrified to realize that I treat prayers like answering a new chain letter every day. Those things are a nuisance. It's almost impossible to believe they do any good. But, if you don't answer one and something bad happens, you'll always wonder if it could have been avoided if you had taken the time to answer that chain letter.

I mean, if you think about the concept of prayer, it's one of the hardest things in the world to really believe in. There's this big guy with unlimited power way away somewhere. Somehow, He is capable of listening to everybody on earth at the very same time, and He pays attention to everybody, too. He can help you with your problems, if He wants to. Now, that is really ridiculous, at least by human standards.

Yet that is at the core of Christianity. I need to face up to it and be honest with myself about whether I believe it or not. Actually, I do believe in God and I do believe in prayer. This is because, in spite of how impossible it seems, I have prayed and gotten miraculous results enough times for me to have a hard time believing it's all a bunch of coincidences. Plus, if there is no God, I'm done for. I really don't have any "Plan B." It's pretty much God or hopelessness for me.

I think I need to ask God to help me pray better. If there was no God, it would not matter how I prayed. But, I am banking on the hope that there is a God. So, shouldn't I respect God the same way I respected the jury in court and try praying the way God said in the Bible that He wants me to pray? I mean, if there is a God, it doesn't seem like it could hurt anything to pray to Him the way He says He wants people to pray to Him in the Bible.

"When you pray, don't be like the hypocrites who love to pray publicly on street corners and in the synagogues where everyone can see them. I tell you the truth, that is all the reward they will ever get. But when you pray, go away by yourself, shut the door behind you, and pray to your Father in private. Then your Father, who sees everything, will reward you.

"When you pray, don't babble on and on and on as the Gentiles do. They think their prayers are answered merely by repeating their words again and again. Don't be like them, for your Father knows exactly what you need even before you ask Him! Pray like this:

"Our Father in Heaven, may your name be kept holy. May your Kingdom come soon. May your will be done on earth, as it is in Heaven. Give us today the food we need, and forgive us our sins, as we have forgiven those

who sin against us. And don't let us yield to temptation, but rescue us from the evil one."

Matthew 6:5-13 (NLT)

Well, if there is a God, and I know there is, that is the kind of prayer He wants to hear. I know that, because the person who said that is Jesus, and He would know.

One of the first Bible verses that I ever knew by heart was this one:

Trust in the Lord with all thine heart; and lean not unto thine own understanding. In all thy ways acknowledge Him, and He shall direct thy paths."
Proverbs 3:5-6 (KJV)

I used to read that as meaning "In all thy ways obey Him, and He shall direct thy paths." But now, I take the word "acknowledge" more seriously. God wants a lot of things from people, but one of the things He really values is being acknowledged by us. He knows that we won't always obey Him. But, I think He thinks there is no excuse for us to not acknowledge Him.

You may disagree with me, and you may be right. But since I do believe that, I must ask myself this question: Am I acknowledging God more by praying to Him the way He says He wants me to pray to Him, or by continuing to pray to Him the way I have been praying to Him, which is pretty much the opposite of how Jesus said I should pray? That is not a very hard question to answer. It might be hard and seem risky for me to break my prayer ritual, but there is no doubt in my mind that I have not been praying the way Jesus wants me to pray.

Dear God, Please help me to have enough faith to stop my superstitious way of praying and to acknowledge you by praying the way you want me to. In Jesus' name, Amen

Message 13

Is My Heart Too Hard?

I have often thought that it is hard for me to believe in Jesus today, because his earthly ministry ended approximately two thousand years ago. But, I always thought that it would have been easy for me to believe in Jesus, if I had just been alive during the time Jesus was conducting his earthly ministry. I could have gone to the Sermon on the Mountain and listened to Him speak. I might have been in one of the crowds that He miraculously fed. Afterwards, I might have gotten to go up to Him and introduce myself to Him, and He might have asked me to be one of his disciples! Then, I would have surely believed, with absolutely no problem and no doubt. Why couldn't I have lived back then, when it was so easy to believe in Jesus?

About this time another large crowd had gathered, and the people ran out of food again. Jesus called his disciples and told them, "I feel sorry for these people. They have been here with me for three days, and they have nothing left to eat. If I send them home hungry, they will faint along the way. For some of them have come a long distance."

His disciples replied, "How are we supposed to find enough food to feed them out here in the wilderness?"

Jesus asked, "How much bread do you have?"

"Seven loaves," they replied.

So Jesus told all the people to sit down on the ground. Then He took the seven loaves, thanked God for them, and broke them into pieces. He gave them to his disciples, who distributed the bread to the crowd. A few small fish were found, too, so Jesus also blessed these and told the disciples to distribute them.

They ate as much as they wanted. Afterward, the

disciples picked up seven large baskets of leftover food.

There were about 4,000 men in the crowd that day, and Jesus sent them home after they had eaten. Immediately after this, He got into a boat with His disciples and crossed over to the region of Dalmanutha.

When the Pharisees heard that Jesus had arrived, they came and started to argue with Him. Testing Him, they demanded that He show them a miraculous sign from Heaven to prove his authority.

When He heard this, He sighed deeply in his spirit and said, "Why do these people keep demanding a miraculous sign? I tell you the truth, I will not give this generation any such sign." So He got back into the boat and left them, and He crossed to the other side of the lake.

But the disciples had forgotten to bring any food. They had only one loaf of bread with them in the boat. As they were crossing the lake, Jesus warned them, "Watch out! Beware of the yeast of the Pharisees and of Herod."

At this they began to argue with each other because they hadn't brought any bread. Jesus knew what they were saying, so He said, "Why are you arguing about having no bread? Don't you know or understand even yet? Are your hearts too hard to take it in? You have eyes—can't you see? You have ears—can't you hear? Don't you remember anything at all? When I fed the 5,000 with five loaves of bread, how many baskets of leftovers did you pick up afterward?"

"Twelve," they said.

"And when I fed the 4,000 with seven loaves, how many large baskets of leftovers did you pick up?"

"Seven," they said.

"Don't you understand yet?" He asked them.

Mark 8:1-21 (NLT)

Well, so much for my theory that it would have been easy for me to believe in Jesus, if I had just lived during his earthly ministry and gotten to be one of his disciples. Even the people who were his disciples had a very hard time believing in Him! They could watch Him feed thousands of people with a few loaves of bread and a few fish, and then be in a boat with Him only a few hours later worrying about not having enough food to eat.

The first time I read the scripture I just quoted, I thought Jesus was asking the Pharisees if their hearts were too hard to recognize Him for who He was. That would have made sense to me. But, I was wrong. Jesus was not talking to the Pharisees when He asked that. Jesus was asking his own disciples if their hearts were too hard to recognize Him for who He was.

I wondered what Jesus meant when He said to his disciples, "Watch out! Beware of the yeast of the

Pharisees and of Herod." I decided that He meant, "You disciples have such little faith. You better watch out, because your doubts about me are close to the doubts about me that the Pharisees and Herod have."

It was never easy to believe in Jesus. It would not have been any easier for me to believe in Jesus if I had been one of his disciples than it is right now. It is very hard to believe in Jesus. But, Jesus knew this better than anybody else.

One day, some parents brought their little children to Jesus so He could touch and bless them. But when the disciples saw this, they scolded the parents for bothering Him.

Then Jesus called for the children and said to the disciples, "Let the children come to me. Don't stop them! For the Kingdom of God belongs to those who are like these children. I tell you the truth, anyone who doesn't receive the Kingdom of God like a child will never enter it."

Luke 18:15-17 (NLT)

If I am having trouble believing in Jesus, I need to ask myself if I'm thinking like an adult or like a child. That's a problem I have. I think like an adult when I'm trying to believe in Jesus. I need to accept Him the way I accepted milk when I was a baby. No questions asked. No second thoughts. No doubts. Just milk.

Dear God, Thank you for showing me in the Bible that even the disciples had trouble believing in Jesus. This encourages me to keep trying. In Jesus' name, Amen

MESSAGE 14

The Holy Spirit

I was raised in a Christian home. Before I was old enough to enter the first grade, I became a member of the McColl, South Carolina Presbyterian Church.

As part of those early church services that I remember so well, the entire congregation would recite or sing a few key things every Sunday.

I will write these down as I remember them, so if I do not get them the way you know them, I apologize.

We would recite The Apostles' Creed.

"I believe in God the Father almighty, maker of Heaven and earth, and in Jesus Christ, His only Son, our Lord, who was conceived of the Holy Spirit and born of the Virgin Mary, who suffered under Pontius Pilate, was crucified, died, and buried, descended into

Hell, rose from the dead, ascended into Heaven, and is seated at the right hand of God the Father almighty, who will come again to judge the quick and the dead. I believe in the Holy Spirit, the holy catholic church, the communion of saints, the forgiveness of sins, the resurrection of the body, and the life everlasting. Amen."

So as not to be misunderstood, I want to say that the reference to the catholic church in lower case is not a reference to The Roman Catholic Church. I was taught that it is a reference to the "universal church." There is no disrespect intended towards The Roman Catholic Church in this distinction.

We would sing two short hymns.

One was The Doxology.

"Praise God, from whom all blessings flow; Praise Him, all creatures here below; Praise Him above, ye Heavenly host; Praise Father, Son, and Holy Ghost. Amen."

The other was The Gloria.

"Glory be to the Father, and to the Son, and to the Holy Ghost; As it was in the beginning, is now, and ever shall be, world without end. Amen. Amen."

I was taught that the Holy Ghost was the same thing as the Holy Spirit. I asked my parents about that because, as a little boy, I didn't want to think there was a ghost flying around in our church.

The sermons changed every week, but these three things never changed. They were the fundamentals of our church.

But, here's my problem. I don't know who or what the Holy Spirit is. I have a rough idea of who God is and who Jesus is. But, I don't know who or what, exactly, the Holy Spirit is.

Of course, that doesn't keep me from talking about the Holy Spirit. For instance, I will say, "I feel like the

Holy Spirit is showing me what to do," or "I can feel the Holy Spirit in my heart today."

When I was young, it didn't bother me that I didn't know exactly what or who the Holy Spirit I recited and sang about every Sunday was. But, now, I am no longer young, and I do want to know. So I tried to find out some things about the Holy Spirit in the Bible.

While Apollos was in Corinth, Paul traveled through the interior regions until he reached Ephesus, on the coast, where he found several believers. "Did you receive the Holy Spirit when you believed?" he asked them.

"No," they replied, "we haven't even heard that there is a Holy Spirit."

"Then what baptism did you experience?" he asked.

And they replied, "The baptism of John."

Paul said, "John's baptism called for repentance from sin. But John himself told the people to believe in the one who would come later, meaning Jesus."

As soon as they heard this, they were baptized in the name of the Lord Jesus. Then, when Paul laid his hands on them, the Holy Spirit came on them, and they spoke in other tongues and prophesied. There were about twelve men in all.

Acts 19:1-7 (NLT)

Afterward Paul felt compelled by the Spirit to go over to Macedonia and Achaia before going to Jerusalem. "And after that," he said, "I must go on to Rome!"

Acts 19:21-22 (NLT)

Then Jesus, full of the Holy Spirit, returned from the Jordan River. He was led by the Spirit in the wilderness.

Luke 4:1 (NLT)

"And do not bring sorrow to God's Holy Spirit by the way you live. Remember, He has identified you as his

own, guaranteeing that you will be saved on the day of redemption." Ephesians 4:30 (NLT)

Jesus came and told his disciples, "I have been given all authority in Heaven and on earth. Therefore go and make disciples of all the nations, baptizing them in the name of the Father and the Son and the Holy Spirit. Teach these new disciples to obey all the commands I have given you. And be sure of this: I am with you always, even to the end of the age."

Matthew 28:18-20 (NLT)

"And now I will send the Holy Spirit, just as my Father promised. But, stay here in the city until the Holy Spirit comes and fills you with power from Heaven."

Then Jesus led them to Bethany, and lifting His hands

to Heaven, He blessed them. While He was blessing them, He left them and was taken up to Heaven.

Luke 24:49-51 (NLT)

So, what did those scriptures tell me about the Holy Spirit?

One, the Holy Spirit was extremely important to Jesus and Paul.

Two, some early Christians didn't even know there was a Holy Spirit. So, if we don't know much about the Holy Spirit, we are not the first Christians who needed to learn.

Three, when these same early Christians were baptized in the name of Jesus, and Paul laid hands on them, the Holy Spirit "came on them."

Four, the Holy Spirit compelled Paul to go to Macedonia and Achaia before going to Jerusalem.

Five, Jesus was full of the Holy Spirit and was led by the Spirit.

Six, the Holy Spirit is the part of God that actually adopts us as His own, guarantees that we will be saved, and is personally hurt when we do wrong.

Seven, the very last thing that Jesus did on earth was to say that He was sending the Holy Spirit to fill Christians with power from Heaven.

This shows me that the Holy Spirit is God's tangible presence, assurance, comfort and direction in and around Christians on earth.

I want to tell you a very true and personal story. About twenty years ago, I was broke, as it seems like I always am. It was the last day on which I could pay the monthly rent of $650.00. If I didn't pay it, my family would be evicted from the house in which we lived. But, I didn't have the money. I had not been able to borrow it.

When I got up that morning, I was very depressed. I walked to the post office to get our mail. There was a letter addressed to me. I opened it. There was a note that only said, "God loves you." There was also a check for exactly $650.00. I saw that it was from a man named Tim Smith. I didn't know who he was. I did some checking. I found out that he was the pastor of Christ Church, an Episcopal church in the town where we were living, Mobile, Alabama.

I had never been to an Episcopal Church, but I decided that I was going to go to that church the next Sunday. That was because I was so thankful to God for what Rev. Smith had done for my family, even though I had absolutely no idea how he had heard of me and my need for that exact amount of money on the exact day it arrived in my post office box.

That Sunday, when I got to the church, everybody was in the fellowship hall. I found Rev. Smith and introduced myself to him. By the time I left the fellowship hall and went into the sanctuary, it was completely full. The only place that I saw to sit was on the very front row, where nobody else was sitting.

I did not know how often the congregation at that church got up, kneeled and sat down during their services. I caught on to the fact that all the people behind me were constantly getting up, kneeling and sitting down. But, it turned out that I spent the whole service getting up when everybody else sat down, sitting down when everybody else got up, and kneeling when everybody else was starting to sing. I could hear their movement behind me, but I could not get in sync with them.

Under normal circumstances, I would have felt terribly embarrassed. But, that day I felt something completely different. I felt a physical glow around my entire body, a feeling that if somebody shot a gun at me, the bullet would just hit the glow I felt around my body and bounce off. I felt totally protected. I knew nothing could possibly hurt me. I never felt that way in my whole life, except for that day. It was beyond amazing and glorious. It was not an emotional feeling. It was a distinctly physical feeling.

But, it only lasted for that hour. The next week, I went back to that church and met with Tim Smith in his office. I described the feeling I had felt in detail to him. I told him that I wanted to have that feeling all the time. I thought that he wouldn't believe me. But, he did. To my great surprise, he knew all about the feeling that I described. He said that it was written up in church literature. Sadly, he told me that I would never feel it again.

That feeling was the Holy Spirit. He had "come on" me.

"After seeing the multitudes, He went up into a mountain: and when He was set, His disciples came

unto Him: And He opened His mouth, and taught them, saying,

"Blessed are the poor in spirit, for theirs is the kingdom of Heaven.

"Blessed are they that mourn: for they shall be comforted."

Matthew 5:1-4 (KJV)

I used to read the Beatitudes and think they were pie in the sky. I used to recite creeds and sing about the Holy Spirit and not even care enough to find out who He was. But, He didn't care if I knew who He was or not. He comforted me. He brought those "pie in the sky" Beatitudes into my life.

Dear God, Thank you so much for the people whose hearts you have miraculously touched to rescue me so many times, and thank you for showing me who the Holy Spirit is. In Jesus' name, Amen

MESSAGE 15

Favored By Life or Favored By God?

In the sixth month of Elizabeth's pregnancy, God sent the angel Gabriel to Nazareth, a village in Galilee, to a virgin named Mary. She was engaged to be married to a man named Joseph, a descendant of King David. Gabriel appeared to her and said, "Greetings, favored woman. The Lord is with you!"

Confused and disturbed, Mary tried to think what the angel could mean. "Don't be afraid, Mary," the angel told her, "for you have found favor with God! You will conceive and give birth to a son, and you will name Him Jesus. He will be very great and will be called the Son of the Most High. The Lord will give Him the throne of His ancestor David. And He will reign over Israel forever; His Kingdom will never end!"

Luke 1:26-33 (NLT)

Scholars estimate that Mary was 13 or 14 when she became pregnant with Jesus. She had fallen in love with Joseph, and they had become engaged. I suspect they felt just as happy and excited about falling in love and getting engaged as people do today. They had plans and dreams, and were looking forward to their life together.

But, their plans were disrupted when Mary was told she was favored by God. Being favored by God caused her to get pregnant while she was engaged and still a virgin. Imagine how she felt when she heard this. Imagine how she felt when she had to tell Joseph about this.

The Bible says that Joseph decided to quietly break off their engagement, so I don't think he believed her story about what the angel had told her. She had to face the prospect of being abandoned by her fiancé and having a very uncertain future. I bet she prayed hard about that. Then, an angel came and convinced Joseph of the truth, and they got married and raised Jesus and his brothers and sisters.

But, the consequences of Mary being favored by God did not end there. Jesus quit being a carpenter when He was thirty and left home to conduct His three year ministry. One time when He came back to the town where He grew up, the people were deeply offended by what He said, refused to believe in Him, and scoffed at Him. I'm sure that was very painful for Mary, and she may have been ridiculed, too.

Then, when it is estimated that Mary was forty-six or forty-seven years old, she watched from the foot of the cross as Jesus was crucified. As far as we know, that was the last time she saw Him on earth.

After He ascended into Heaven, we read of her for the last time. The Bible says she was doing the same thing she was doing when she was first favored by God. She was praying, probably in desperation and sadness.

So, all that excruciating pain and anguish was the result of her being favored by God. I'm sure she had some happy times that we don't know about, but her life certainly had challenges, heart-break and confusion.

Yet, she showed the character that attracted God's favor. When told that she was going to have Jesus, her brave response was to tell the angel, "I am the Lord's servant. May everything you have said about me come true." Thirty-three years later, when this son she had been told about was despised and crucified, Mary was right there at the foot of the cross to look into his eyes as He died.

So, this is what we can expect if we are favored by God. But, this story is very encouraging to me. It means that no matter how depressing things get, no matter how much duct tape you have to put on your old worn out sitting chair, no matter how old your car is, no matter how bad you feel, no matter how uncertain your future on earth is, and no matter how far your life has spun out of control and away from what you imagined it would be, it does not mean that you have been abandoned by God. In fact, it may mean you have been favored by God! So, we must keep doing the best we can and trusting God, even when things are confusing and depressing.

The point is that we can have a life that is full of all imaginable earthly blessings, success, wealth and excellent health without ever giving a thought to God. We may think we are very happy and have everything under control. We may feel sorry for people we know who are gossiped about because "they had to get married," or have a child who is tried, convicted and executed by the government, or have to rely on charity to have a place to live and even for food to eat because they failed to succeed in this life and could not take care of themselves financially. We may even thank God we are not like such pitiful people.

But, watch out! The people we consider the most pathetic may be the most favored by God. The people we think have failed in life may actually appear that way because God has favored them and is using them for a special purpose.

We must never think that being considered successful in life means that we are favored by God. And we also must never think that being favored by God means that we will be considered successful in life.

Dear God, When I see somebody who has not been favored by life, help me to remember the story of Mary. Help me to respect the fact that the most humble person on earth may be the most favored person in Heaven. In Jesus' name, Amen

The Ultimate Compliment

For many years, I was a criminal defense lawyer. Most of my clients were indigent defendants, whom judges appointed me to represent. There was a feeling among many of these defendants that a lawyer who was appointed by a judge and paid for by the state was really working for the government and not for them. This was a layer of distrust that was hard to overcome.

I noticed that one thing I said to these defendants when I met with them at the jail for the first time always broke down the distrust that they felt towards me. But, I did not say it to get their trust. I said it because I sincerely wanted their help.

This is what made such a big difference in my relationships with them. I would say, "I will do all I can to help you, and I will ask God to take charge of your case and guide us in what we do together while we are working on it. But, there is something very important that I need for you to do for me, too. I need you to pray for my wife, my family, and me every day and every night. You might be locked in this jail, but you still have the power to do that for me. And it is the most important and powerful thing that anybody could ever do for me."

These people were very discouraged. They were in a situation that is hard to describe. They had no control over their own lives. Most of them felt full of guilt and regret. They didn't think there was anything they could do for anybody from where they were. They could not envision any future for themselves.

Then, I would tell them a summary of the following scripture.

"But when the Son of Man comes in his glory, and all the angels with Him, then He will sit upon his glorious throne. All the nations will be gathered in his presence, and He will separate the people as a shepherd separates the sheep and the goats. He will place the sheep at His right hand and the goats at His left.

"Then, the King will say to those on his right, 'Come, you who are blessed by my Father, inherit the Kingdom prepared for you from the creation of the world. For I was hungry, and you fed me. I was thirsty, and you gave me a drink. I was a stranger, and you invited me into your home. I was naked, and you gave me clothing. I was sick, and you cared for me. I was in prison, and you visited me.'

"Then these righteous ones will reply, 'Lord, when did we ever see you hungry and feed you? Or thirsty and give you something to drink? Or a stranger and show *you hospitality? Or naked and give you clothing? When did we ever see you sick or in prison and visit you?'*

"And the King will say, 'I tell you the truth, when you did it to the least of these my brothers and sisters, you were doing it to me!'"

Matthew 25:31-40 (NLT)

I would then look into their eyes and say, "You see, when I look into your eyes, I am not seeing you. I am seeing Jesus. That is what this verse tells me to do, and it also tells me that people in jail are very important to Him. That's why He mentioned them in this scripture. So, you can be sure that when you pray from inside this jail, your prayers will be very powerful, and hearing your prayers will be very important to God. That's why I want you to pray for my wife, my family, and me so much.

"Jesus is watching me right now to see how I treat you. If I don't treat you the right way, it will be me, and not you, that will lose the most from this case."

I guess they could see and feel how sincere I was. I could see a change in them. It seemed like I could see the scales of distrust falling from their eyes. After that, I never had a problem getting their trust again. They trusted me, and I cared about them. We actually became friends.

It wasn't until I had experienced this many times with many defendants that I asked myself why this conversation had such a powerful impact on my relationships with these people. When I thought about it, I realized what was going on. When you ask somebody to pray for you, you are actually paying them the ultimate compliment. You are telling them that they have worth to both God and to you, and that God cares about them and what they say in their prayers to Him.

I also sadly and vividly recall something that taught me the powerful impact of having somebody ask me to pray for him. After my Daddy had his second operation for cancer, I watched as he was brought from the operating room to his bed in the glass walled intensive care unit of the Peach County Hospital in Fort Valley, Georgia.

Then, I watched his doctor go in and talk to my Daddy about the results of his operation. When the doctor finished talking with Daddy, he saw me standing and waiting to talk with him. The doctor came over to me and said, "Son, the cancer has spread. We cannot remove it. There is nothing we can do to cure your father, and I have just given him that news." Then, he said that I could go into the intensive care unit and talk with my Daddy.

I was nervous and sad. I didn't have any idea what to say. When I opened the door to my Daddy's room, he looked at me and simply said, "Pray for me." I never felt so small and humble in all my life. For my entire life, my Daddy had been the person I went to when I needed advice or help. He had never let me down. But, now, this man on whom I had always depended was asking me to pray for him. I don't even remember what I said. I don't think life was ever quite the same to me again.

But even in such a sad hour, my Daddy had paid me the ultimate compliment. He had told me that I had worth to both God and to him. His faith outshone his grief.

Dear God, Help me to always remember that you are watching how I treat people. Help me to treat them like I would treat you. In Jesus' name, Amen

MESSAGE 17

Matthew

Besides Jesus, some of the names that come to my mind the most when I think about Christianity are Matthew, Mark, Luke and John. That is because I think of these men as the biographers of Jesus. It is from their writings that the most words and thoughts of Jesus are available to me.

So, I became interested in finding out a little about these men. I never went to a seminary and do not claim to be an expert on these men's lives, but the following brief summary of what I have learned about Matthew is interesting and helpful to me. I realize some scholars may disagree with some parts of it.

Before Jesus called Matthew to become one of His disciples, Matthew was a tax collector. There were a lot abuses in the tax collecting system of the day. While the position of being a tax collector was a highly lucrative one, it was not a respected one. Tax collectors were considered greedy and even extortionists. Sometimes, tax collectors needed to take Roman soldiers with them for protection when they went around trying to collect unjustly high taxes.

I like to think of Matthew as having been educated to be an accountant, because my Daddy was an accountant. In his writing, Matthew stressed that Jesus fulfilled Old Testament prophecies. He wrote his Gospel to specifically appeal to his fellow Jews, hoping they would read it and become Christians, just as he had become a Christian.

Matthew was one of the original twelve disciples of Jesus. However, according to his own account, he was not called by Jesus to be a disciple as early as some of the others. In fact, Matthew indicates that he was not called to follow Jesus until after The Sermon on the Mountain, even though he reports that sermon in his Gospel.

Matthew, who is also referred in the Bible as Levi, records his own calling this way:

As Jesus was walking along, He saw a man named Matthew sitting at his tax collector's booth. "Follow me and be my disciple," Jesus said to him. So, Matthew got up and followed Him.

Later, Matthew invited Jesus and his disciples to his home as dinner guests, along with many tax collectors and other disreputable sinners. But, when the Pharisees saw this, they asked his disciples, "Why does your teacher eat with such scum?"

When Jesus heard this, He said, "Healthy people don't need a doctor—sick people do." Then He added, "Now go and learn the meaning of this Scripture: 'I want you to show mercy, not offer sacrifices.' For I have come to call not those who think they are righteous, but those who know they are sinners."

Matthew 9:9-13 (NLT)

Mark and Luke have similar accounts of Jesus calling Matthew to become a disciple. Luke makes it clear that Matthew gave Jesus "a great feast in his own house."

Why would Matthew give such a great feast for Jesus after Jesus called Matthew to become one of His disciples? I don't know for sure, but I think it was because Matthew knew that while being a tax collector had made him financially rich, it had also made him morally poor. I think Matthew was extremely grateful to Jesus for being willing to take him, a terrible sinner, as a disciple. I think Matthew wanted to celebrate this transformation of his life with his old friends and former colleagues, so they might sense his joy and be motivated to change their lives and commit themselves to Jesus, just as Matthew had done.

The last thing Matthew wrote in his gospel was The Great Commission.

Then the eleven disciples left for Galilee, going to the mountain where Jesus had told them to go. When they saw Him, they worshipped Him—but some of them doubted!

Jesus came and told His disciples, "I have been given all authority in Heaven and on earth. Therefore, go and make disciples of all the nations, baptizing them in the name of the Father and the Son and the Holy Spirit. Teach these new disciples to obey all the commands I have given you. And be sure of this: I am with you always, even to the end of the age."

Matthew 28:16-20 (NLT)

Dear God, Thank you for the great encouragement I feel when I hear Jesus saying, "I have come to call not those who think they are righteous, but those who know they are sinners." This means the world to me. In Jesus' name, Amen

MESSAGE 18

Money or Faith

Someone came to Jesus with a question: "Teacher, what good deed must I do to have eternal life?"

"Why ask me about what is good?" Jesus replied. "There is only one who is good. But to answer your question—if you want to receive eternal life, keep the commandments."

"Which ones?" the man asked.

And Jesus replied: "'You must not murder. You must not commit adultery. You must not steal. You must not testify falsely. Honor your father and mother. Love your neighbor as yourself.'"

"I've obeyed all these commandments," the young man replied. "What else must I do?"

Jesus told him, "If you want to be perfect, go and

sell all your possessions and give the money to the poor, and you will have treasure in Heaven. Then come, follow me."

But when the young man heard this, he went away sad, for he had many possessions.

Then Jesus said to the disciples, "I tell you the truth, it is very hard for a rich person to enter the Kingdom of Heaven. I'll say it again—it is easier for a camel to go through the eye of a needle than for a rich person to enter the Kingdom of God!"

Matthew 19:16-24 (NLT)

I have read this passage many times in my life. But, it wasn't until tonight that the Holy Spirit showed me what it really means.

The story began when the young man asked Jesus, "What deed must I do to have eternal life?" Jesus could have told him that it is impossible for people to earn eternal life through good deeds. But, Jesus took a different approach and said, "To answer your question—if you want to receive eternal life, keep the commandments."

The young man replied, "Which ones?" This must have been amusing to Jesus. He could have said, "They're all God's commandments. If He didn't want you to keep them all, He wouldn't have given them to you."

But, Jesus didn't say that. He said, "You must not murder. You must not commit adultery. You must not steal. You must not testify falsely. Honor your father and mother. Love your neighbor as yourself."

This is an interesting list. It includes five of the Ten Commandments and one of the two commandments Jesus said were the most important. To believe that Jesus really took this man's question as anything other than ridiculous, we would have to believe that Jesus only thought five of the Ten Commandments and one thing from His own teaching were important. Obviously, that is not true.

The young man told Jesus, "I've obeyed all these commandments. What else must I do?"

Jesus answered that if the young man wanted to be perfect, he had to sell all of his possessions, give the money he received from selling them to the poor, and then come and follow Him. The Bible says that the young man "went away sad, for he had many possessions."

As the young man was walking away, Jesus said to his disciples, "It is very hard for a rich person to enter the Kingdom of Heaven."

But, what did Jesus mean by "rich"? Based on reading and thinking about the entire passage, I don't think Jesus meant "wealthy." I think Jesus was talking about people in all income brackets who are so attached to their possessions that they would rather keep them than to give them up if Jesus asked them to do so. I think this entire passage is designed to make all of us examine our priorities.

As I write this, I have two Bibles beside me. One of them has this passage under the heading, "Jesus Counsels The Rich Young Ruler." The other has this passage under the heading, "The Rich Man." So, the popular emphasis given to this story focuses on the rich.

Matthew, Mark and Luke give different descriptions of the young man in this passage, and some translations describe him differently, too. In the NASB translation, Matthew and Mark do not say the young man in the story was either rich or a ruler, but they do say he "owned much property." The NLT translation of Luke describes him as a "religious leader" and "very rich." The NASB translation of

Luke, describes as a "ruler" and as "extremely rich." Other translations offer other descriptions of him.

From all these different accounts, I don't think there is a consensus description of this man. But, it does not really matter to me whether he was an extremely rich religious leader or a man who had many possessions. I believe the story is about establishing priorities in our lives, particularly between our material possessions and our faith.

Would we really rather lose our money or our faith? That's the big question every person must face, and that's the question the young man in this passage is asked by Jesus. It is very wrong to think Jesus is only asking this question to rich people.

When I represented indigent defendants when I was a lawyer, I often visited their homes. Some of these homes were very depressing to me. It seemed like the people were living in total poverty and that they didn't have hardly anything. But, then I looked closer. They did have things. Their TVs were on, their children were all clutching a toy or a doll, they had furniture, they had food, they had a car, they had a place to call home, and they had a Bible. Their possessions were just as important to them as my possessions are to me.

I never represented any indigent who didn't want to get back to his home and his possessions just as much as rich clients wanted to get back to their homes and their possessions. So, this question that Jesus is asking is no easier to answer for the poor than it is for the rich. Your money or your faith, which would you really choose to wake up tomorrow morning without?

At least the young man in this story was honest. He was talking person-to-person and face-to-face with Jesus! But, when he heard this question, he turned around and walked away from Jesus. In effect, he said,

"I'm sorry, but I'd rather have my possessions." He probably never saw Jesus again.

There is one more question that is sort of implied in this passage. That question is: Should we all sell everything we have right now and give it to the poor? I don't think that is what the passage is telling us to do. I think the passage is telling us to be ready at all times to use our talents and resources in any way God tells us we should.

A good example of this is given in the New Testament, itself.

Soon afterward Jesus began a tour of the nearby towns and villages, preaching and announcing the Good News about the Kingdom of God. He took his twelve disciples with Him, along with some women who had been cured of evil spirits and diseases. Among them were Mary Magdalene, from whom He had cast out seven demons; Joanna, the wife of Chuza, Herod's business manager; Susanna; and many others who were contributing from their own resources to support Jesus and his disciples.

Luke 8:1-3 (NLT)

To a large extent, Jesus' earthly ministry relied on the support of people who had financial resources. If these people had not accumulated resources, they would not have been able to provide the support that Jesus and his disciples needed. They did the right thing to keep their resources until God told them how He wanted them to be used.

Dear God, Thank You for showing me the big question you have for me in this passage. If I ever have to choose between you and everything I possess, help me to choose you. In Jesus' name, Amen

Message 19

Repentance

During my life, I never wanted to hurt people. But, I have been selfish, and as a result I have hurt many people.

When I sinned, I did not see all the people I was hurting. I'm sure that as I look back on my life, I have no idea of all the people I have hurt or how badly I have hurt them. When I sinned, I only thought of my selfish desires and the people who seemed to be enjoying my sins with me. I didn't want to think about the people I was hurting.

But, my sins had unintended consequences. They hurt people I never thought about or didn't even know about. I hate to think about all the people I have hurt through my selfish sins, including the people in my own family. I knew I was sinning, but I was too selfish to think about the consequences of what I was doing on other people.

I guess I spent my whole life thinking God must grade on the curve. I mean, I was falling short of what He wanted me to do, but I thought I was pretty good compared to a lot of other people.

And I loved my sins, too. When I prayed, I was actually foolish enough to say, "I ask you to forgive me for my sins and for my sinfulness." I thought God would give me credit for being sort of honest with Him. I repented for my sins that I really didn't want to commit anymore. Then, I repented for what I called "my sinfulness," meaning the sins I liked too much to give up.

Then, I wondered why I had low self-esteem and wasn't successful, and why people didn't respect me more. Yes, I cared about people, I witnessed to people, and I tried hard to help people. But, I held on to my favorite sins. I would not surrender them. I thought God would see that I was a pretty nice person and not hold my sins against me.

But, I was a fool. I ignored all the scriptures that were there to tell me that I was a fool.

Dear friends, if we deliberately continue sinning after we have received knowledge of the truth, there is no longer any sacrifice that will cover these sins.

Hebrews 10:26 (NLT)

I also ignored the scriptures that warned me that God definitely did not grade on the curve.

"Enter by the narrow gate; for wide is the gate and broad is the way that leads to destruction, and there are many who go in by it. Because narrow is the gate and

difficult is the way which leads to life, and there are few who find it."

Matthew 7:13-14 (NKJV)

I was always smart. I think I did a lot of things that God liked, such as praying with prisoners in jail. Most of the time, I was very nice to people, too. But, these scriptures say I was headed to Hell!

So, what could I do to avoid the horrible fate I so clearly deserved? Well, nothing! No matter how hard I tried, I would never have been able to lead a life that met the requirements to enter through the narrow gate that leads to salvation.

That is where Jesus' death on the cross saved me.

For God so loved the world, that He gave his only begotten Son, that whosoever believeth in Him should not perish, but have everlasting life. For God sent not his son into the world to condemn the world; but that the world through Him might be saved. He that believeth on Him is not condemned: but he that believeth not is condemned already, because he hath not believed in the name of the only begotten Son of God.

John 3:16-18 (KJV)

The good news is that I will be forgiven if I believe in Jesus. But, the bad news is that I can't get back all the things I lost by sinning, and I can't erase the hurt I caused so many people by sinning.

However, I can commit myself to trying my best to live the way Jesus taught us to live for the rest of my life. I will still fail, and I will still only be saved by believing in Jesus. But, I will have the life God wants me to have for the rest of my life. I will have self-respect. I won't hurt more people, and I won't hurt the people I have already hurt even more.

I wish I had made that decision when I was young

and stayed committed to it all my life. I still would have failed to be sinless and I still would have needed to believe in Jesus to be saved. But, I would have had a much better life and hurt a lot less people.

Dear God, Thank you for saving me from the fate I deserved. Thank you for letting me be saved by believing in Jesus. Please help me to live like you want me to for the rest of my life. And please comfort the many people I have hurt. In Jesus' name, Amen

Message 20

Hope

When I think of Christianity, I think of faith. But, life is not simple enough for that to work, and Christianity is not that simple, either. There has got to be more for me in Christianity than just faith, because sometimes life overwhelms me, and I don't really have any faith. Faith temporarily fails me, or I fail it. When my faith disappears, I need something else from God to put in its place.

When this happens, I think I have failed. I think, "No real Christian would ever lose his faith." But, there is no denying that I do lose my faith sometimes. Still, I think that God understood this was going happen, and that He prepared something to get me through those times.

Three things will last forever—faith, hope, and love—and the greatest of these is love.

1 Corinthians 13:13 (NLT)

When I read that scripture and think about it, I feel sort of amazed that God said hope was one of the things that will last forever. Why would He think I needed hope, once I had faith? I think it's because He knows how weak my faith is and how extremely hard it is for me to have faith all the time.

"You don't have enough faith," Jesus told them. "I tell you the truth, if you had faith even as small as a mustard seed, you could say to this mountain, 'Move from here to there,' and it would move. Nothing would be impossible."

Matthew 17:20-21 (NLT)

Since I believe what Jesus said and would love to help people believe in Jesus, I would certainly be moving mountains instead of writing these messages, if I could. But, I can't, because I don't have enough faith.

But, does that disqualify me from serving God?

After they gathered again in Galilee, Jesus told them, "The Son of Man is going to be betrayed into the hands of his enemies. He will be killed, but on the third day He will be raised from the dead." And the disciples were filled with grief.

Matthew 17:22-23 (NLT)

Now, I would expect that after having spent so much time with Jesus and having seen Him do so many miracles, the disciples would have believed what Jesus told them and would have been expecting Him to be raised from the dead on the third day after He was crucified. But, they didn't even have enough faith in Jesus to believe what He told them face-to-face.

After Jesus rose from the dead early on Sunday morning, the first person who saw Him was Mary Magdalene, the woman from whom He had cast out seven demons. She went to the disciples, who were grieving and weeping, and told them what had happened. But when she told them that Jesus was alive and she had seen Him, they didn't believe her.

Mark 16:9-11 (NLT)

This passage encourages me when my faith wanes. That is because, even though the disciples didn't have enough faith to believe that Jesus had done exactly what He had told them He was going to do, He still loved them and used them to start the process of taking his message to the entire world.

I wasn't there with them when they didn't have

the faith necessary to believe that Jesus had risen. But, I am sure they at least had hope that what Mary Magdalene was telling them was the truth.

During World War II, my Uncle Lykes Henderson was the pilot of a U.S. Army Air Corps bomber. He was stationed in England. One day, he flew a mission to Germany. On the way back to England, his plane was shot down over France. The nine members of his crew parachuted to safety. But Uncle Lykes could not parachute, because he had been hit in his head by flack.

So, he brought his plane down miles away from where his crew members had parachuted. His nine crew members were found by the Germans together in one place, put in a POW camp, and reported by the Red Cross as being prisoners of war. But, since Uncle Lykes was not with them, he was reported to my Aunt Ruth as being missing in action, which meant that he was presumed to be dead. My Aunt Ruth could not have faith that He was alive. But she fiercely held on to her hope that he was alive and would come home to her. She said she felt that way because Uncle Lykes had promised her that he would come back.

It turned out that Uncle Lykes was found by another German unit, taken to a hospital for operations, and then put in a POW camp. Eventually, my Aunt Ruth got wonderful news. She was informed in a telegram that my Uncle Lykes was no longer missing in action. He was a prisoner of war.

Even when there was no reason for hope, Abraham kept hoping—believing that he would become the father of many nations. For God had said to him, "That's how many descendants you will have!"

Romans 4:18 (NLT)

This is a very special verse to me. It tells me that there are times in our lives when we just have to hold on, even when we do not know what we are holding on for. Sometimes, when there is no reason for hope, we have to keep on hoping. For example, Winston Churchill led England to do this at the start of World War II.

Now faith is the substance of things hoped for, the evidence of things not seen.

Hebrews 11:1 (KJV)

God gave us hope to sustain us when we are unable to have faith. But hope is not just a temporary substitute for faith. It is also a stepping stone on the road to faith.

For we have heard of your faith in Christ Jesus and your love for all of God's people, which come from your confident hope of what God has reserved for you in

Heaven. You have had this expectation ever since you first heard the truth of the Good News.

Colossians 1:4-5 (NLT)

Paul said faith and love come from hope. So, there are those three wonderful things again: Hope, faith and love.

Dear God, Thank you for acknowledging the importance of hope. In Jesus' name, Amen

Message 21

Worship

I write these messages after my wife goes to bed at night. On some nights I have no idea what I am going to write about. This was one of those nights. I talked to my wife about what I could write about. I thought about it. I tracked down some thoughts I had in the Bible. But, nothing was happening. I didn't feel like I had anything.

Finally, I just prayed and asked God what He wanted me to write about. From out of absolutely nowhere, the word "worship" popped into my head. Right away I got that exciting feeling I get when I feel like I'm connecting with God. "OK," I thought, "Tonight, I will write about worship."

The first thing that came into my mind was, "Why should I worship? What do I get out of it? It doesn't do anything for me. I'm more interested in more practical things."

Then, the Holy Spirit spoke to my heart. "It's not supposed to help you, Steve. Worship is something that you can do to help me."

I thought about a scripture that illustrates this.

One of the Pharisees asked Jesus to have dinner with him, so Jesus went to his home and sat down to eat. When a certain immoral woman from that city heard He was eating there, she brought a beautiful alabaster jar filled with expensive perfume. Then she knelt behind Him at his feet, weeping. Her tears fell on his feet, and she wiped them off with her hair. Then she kept kissing his feet and putting perfume on them.

When the Pharisee who had invited Him saw this, he said to himself, "If this man were a prophet, He would know what kind of woman is touching Him. She's a sinner!"

Then Jesus answered his thoughts. "Simon," He said to the Pharisee, "I have something to say to you."

"Go ahead, Teacher," Simon replied.

Then Jesus told him this story: "A man loaned money to two people—500 pieces of silver to one and 50 pieces to the other. But neither of them could repay him, so he kindly forgave them both, cancelling their debts. Who do you suppose loved him more after that?"

Simon answered, "I suppose the one for whom he cancelled the larger debt."

"That's right," Jesus said. Then He turned to the woman and said to Simon, "Look at this woman kneeling here. When I entered your home, you didn't

offer me water to wash the dust from my feet, but she has washed them with her hair. You didn't greet me with a kiss, but from the time I first came in, she has not stopped kissing my feet. You neglected the courtesy of olive oil to anoint my head, but she has anointed my feet with rare perfume.

"I tell you, her sins—and they are many—have been forgiven, so she has shown me much love. But a person who is forgiven little shows only little love." Then Jesus said to the woman, "Your sins are forgiven."

The men at the table said among themselves, "Who is this man, that He goes around forgiving sins?"

And Jesus said to the woman, "Your faith has saved you; go in peace." Luke 7:36-50 (NLT)

When I thought carefully about this scripture, I saw something that was important to me. This lady did not do all this for Jesus in order to get forgiven. I say this because Jesus said, "I tell you, her sins—and they are many—have been forgiven, so she has shown me much love." That and the parable Jesus told make it clear to me that Jesus' forgiveness of this lady came before she brought the expensive perfume to where Jesus was, got His feet wet with her tears, and dried them with her hair.

I know Jesus said He forgave her again at the end of this scripture. But, I believe that was just to let the other people there hear Him say what He had already told her.

None of these acts of love were performed by this lady to get anything. She already had the forgiveness she had wanted and needed from Jesus. These acts of pure worship were performed by this lady for only one reason: To comfort Jesus!

That's what makes worship different from other types of interaction with God. In the other types of interaction with God, such as prayer, we are asking God for something. But in worship, we are not asking God for anything. Our sole purpose in worship is to give comfort to God.

However, it was inevitable that, when Jesus saw that this lady had sought Him out just to comfort Him, his affection for her increased. Our friendship with Jesus is affected by the same things that affect our friendships with others.

Mark adds a tribute that Jesus paid to this lady. It shows how much her kindness meant to Him.

"I tell you the truth, wherever the Good News is preached throughout the world, this woman's deed will be remembered and discussed."

Mark 14:9 (NLT)

Our worship is very appreciated by God. He needs comfort, just as the Bible says He needed a day of rest after He worked six days to create the world. God's needs are surprisingly similar to our own.

The following similar story shows how much Jesus appreciates a friend just taking the time to listen to Him.

As Jesus and His disciples continued on their way to Jerusalem, they came to a certain village where a woman named Martha welcomed Him to her home. Her sister, Mary, sat at the Lord's feet, listening to what He taught. But Martha was distracted by the big dinner she was preparing. She came to Jesus and said, "Lord, doesn't it seem unfair to you that my sister just sits here while I do all the work? Tell her to come and help me."

But the Lord said to her, "My dear Martha, you are worried and upset over all these details! There is only one thing worth being concerned about. Mary has discovered it, and it will not be taken away from her."

Luke 10:38-42 (NLT)

Dear God, Help me to remember why worship is so important to you, and that it is you who it is meant to comfort. In Jesus' name, Amen

MESSAGE 22

Why Jacob had to Wrestle God

Jacob was returning to his home. But, the Bible says Jacob was terrified that his brother, Esau, was coming with an army of men to attack him and his family. The first thing Jacob did in his fear was to pray.

"O Lord, please rescue me from the hand of my brother, Esau. I am afraid that he is coming to attack me, along with my wives and children. But you promised me, 'I will surely treat you kindly, and I will multiply your descendants until they become as numerous as the sands along the seashore—too many to count.'"

Genesis 32:11-12 (NLT)

So, the first thing Jacob did to seek help for his distress was to talk with God about his fear. He did not think he could handle his problems on his own, so he begged God to rescue him.

This was the most important and desperate prayer of Jacob's life. But, God did not answer it as soon as Jacob wanted Him to. In Jacob's mind, it was an unanswered prayer in the middle of a dire emergency. So, Jacob lost his confidence that God would answer his prayer. Jacob did not have the faith to trust God to keep His word to protect him or to wait for God to answer his prayer. Instead, Jacob gave in to his fear and started doing things on his own, including evacuating his family and his possessions from his camp.

Jacob had made a terrible mistake. There are no unanswered prayers. There are, however, many prayers that God does not answer in the way we expect or at the time we expect.

Nonetheless, God kept his word to Jacob, even

though it must have hurt God that Jacob did not keep his faith in Him. The Bible tells what happened next.

This left Jacob all alone in the camp, and a man came and wrestled with him until the dawn began to break. When the man saw that He would not win the match, he touched Jacob's hip and wrenched it out of its socket. Then the man said, "Let me go, for the dawn is breaking!"

But Jacob said, "I will not let you go unless You bless me."

"What is your name?" the man asked.

He replied, "Jacob."

"Your name will no longer be Jacob," the man told him. "From now on you will be called Israel, because you have fought with God and with men and have won."

"Please tell me your name," Jacob said.

"Why do you want to know my name?" the man replied. Then He blessed Jacob there.

Jacob named the place Peniel (which means "face of God"), for he said, "I have seen God face to face, yet my life has been spared." The sun was rising as Jacob left Peniel, and he was limping because of the injury to his hip.

Genesis 32:24-31 (NLT)

This is the way I interpret this story. Jacob was in deep worry over his situation. He prayed and asked God to rescue him, but when God did not answer his prayer in the way or at the time he had hoped God would, Jacob gave in to his fear and took matters into his own hands. He moved his family and possessions into a place where he thought they would be safe, instead of leaving them where they were and trusting that God to keep them safe. Then, Jacob returned to his camp, to await whatever was going to happen alone.

At this point, I believe God wanted to teach Jacob a lesson about faith. So, instead of just giving Jacob the blessing he needed, He made Jacob fight for it. God came into Jacob's camp and made Jacob wrestle with Him all night. Certainly God would have had no trouble winning this wrestling match if He had wanted to. But, God did not want to win. He wanted Jacob to have to wrestle with Him all night to get the blessing that God always intended to give him.

I don't think all this wrestling was physical. I think most of it was spiritual. Jacob had to wrestle in his mind with his thoughts about the faithfulness of God. Only when Jacob came to the knowledge that his only chance to achieve security was to hold on to God in all situations did God give him his blessing. The Bible says that, even after experiencing the excruciating pain of having his hip dislocated, Jacob would not let go of God. Jacob told God that he would not let go of Him until God blessed him. Then, God changed Jacob's name to Israel. I think this was because Jacob had shown the high degree to which he acknowledged his need for God. After this, God blessed Jacob, as the sun rose signaling a new time in Jacob's relationship with God.

The message I get from this story is that, when I feel overwhelmed, I should pray. If I don't get an answer in my heart like I usually do, I should not take that to mean that God has abandoned me, because He promised He would never do that.

For the Lord will not abandon his people, Nor will He abandon his inheritance.

Psalm 94:14 (NASB)

The Lord will not abandon his people, because that would dishonor his great name. For it has pleased the Lord to make you his very own people.

1 Samuel 12:22 (NLT)

If one of my prayers is not answered in the way God usually answers my prayers, I should have confidence that He will answer that prayer in a different way. I must not doubt that God has heard my prayer, and I must not doubt that He will answer my prayer at a time and in a manner that He knows is best for me.

Dear God, If my prayers are not answered as soon as I hope they will be or in the way I hope they will be, help me to keep my confidence in you. In Jesus' name, Amen

MESSAGE 23

Fear

My life has been absolutely full of fear for as long as I can remember. I have never had one day that hasn't included fear.

When I was born, I was not taken home. I was sent to an orphanage. It was part of God's plan for me to be adopted by the two people that I know God intended to be my Momma and Daddy. They loved my sister and me and sacrificed for us as much as any biological parents ever could. Still, I never, ever got over being adopted. It was not very often on the front of my mind, but it was always very much alive in my mind somewhere.

I was four years old when my Momma and Daddy decided to adopt a little girl. So that I would feel included in this, they took me with them when they went back to the orphanage where they had gotten me to get my sister. I still remember this very vividly. Momma, Daddy and I were sitting in a room. Then, a nice lady who was in charge of the whole process came in and sat with us.

Next, they brought in three pastel colored bassinettes. Each one of them contained a baby girl. The lady in charge said, "Now, Stevie, walk over there and pick out your sister." I was very uncomfortable in this situation, but I did what the lady said. I walked over to the bassinettes, looked down at the baby girls in them, and quickly picked the one in the middle. She immediately became my sister, Sally.

A few minutes later, Momma, Daddy, Sally and I were leaving the orphanage to get in the car and go home. As we were walking out of the room where all of this had happened, the nice lady who had asked me to pick out my sister said something to Momma and Daddy. I still remember it very well. She said, "If this baby doesn't work out, just bring her back and we'll give you another one." She may have just been joking, but what she said made me think that, if I didn't work out, Momma and Daddy could bring me back to the orphanage and get a replacement for me, too.

Then and there, I had a debilitating element of insecurity and fear put into my life. It took up all the space in my heart and mind that should have been filled with the assurance of unconditional love. But, how could I feel unconditional love in a world in which I thought I could be returned to an orphanage by my parents and replaced by another child if I didn't "work out"?

I could have possibly gotten over this fear if I had talked with my parents about it. But, I never even one time in all my life ever mentioned adoption to my parents. I was afraid that if I did, they would think I didn't think they were my real parents. The last thing on earth that I wanted to do was to hurt their feelings. So, this fear took root and grew in my heart and mind. I equated "not working out" with "being bad" and deserving to be "punished."

Unfortunately, my inability to believe in unconditional love spread into my thoughts about my relationship with God. I could not believe that God could love me unconditionally, either. After all, I have done and still do so many things that displease Him. How could He possibly keep on loving me forever? I came to believe that I really deserved to be punished by God in the worst way possible. My life came down to expecting during some time of every day that this could be the time when God would punish me for all I had done wrong.

I still feel that terrible fear of inevitably receiving

the horrible punishment from God which I fully deserve. To me, it's not a matter of whether God will punish me. It's a matter only of when and how God will punish me. This has devastated me all my life. All I knew to do about it was to stay busy doing things so that I could be distracted from thinking about it. But, I never had a day when I was so distracted that I didn't find time to think about the inevitability of being punished by God.

The worst thing is that I didn't think God's punishment would come in the form of something terrible happening to me. I always imagined that God would punish me by causing something bad to happen to people in my family. These are people who are so important to me that I would much rather die, myself, than to try to live without them.

If you are a well-adjusted person, you may be reading this and not understand how I feel. But, if there is anybody reading this that identifies with any of the feelings I have expressed, I want to tell you something. I know the very deep emotional pain you are living with. I know it haunts your existence every single day and steals your chance for joy. I respect your pain. God does, too, and He loves you just as much as He loves anybody else on earth. Don't look for the answer to your feelings just from psychologists, psychiatrists and medicine. Those good people and medical treatments may be able to help you, but only God can heal you. I know that this is true.

So, I have laid out the problem. But, two things are missing. Where is this fear coming from, and how can I get rid of it? Tonight, while I was thinking about writing this, the Holy Spirit led me to two scriptures that explained these things to me.

Here they are:

Such love has no fear, because perfect love expels all

fear. If we are afraid, it is for fear of punishment, and this shows that we have not fully experienced his perfect love.

1 John 4:18 (NLT)

"When an evil spirit leaves a person, it goes into the desert, seeking rest but finding none. Then it says, 'I will return to the person I came from.' So it returns and finds its former home empty, swept, and in order. Then the spirit finds seven other spirits more evil than itself, and they all enter the person and live there. And so that person is worse off than before. That will be the experience of this evil generation."

Matthew 12:43-45 (NLT)

I have quoted these scriptures above, but now let me tell you what the Holy Spirit told me after I read them.

"Steve, the love that God has for you is truly unconditional. It does not contain a single element of fear. God has no punishment in store for you, so quit fearing it. Quit fearing God! Your problem is not that God doesn't love you enough. Your problem is that you won't accept the unconditional love that God has for you.

"That lady back at that orphanage was not speaking for God. The Devil used her words to mess up your life. That is where your fear came from. Banish what she said and everything that grew out of it from every part of your heart and mind. Then, immediately fill all those parts of your heart and mind, which the Devil's thoughts had been in, with the unconditional love of God. That is how you can get rid of your fear.

"But remember, if you don't immediately accept God's unconditional love, the Devil's fear will come back into your life. That false fear of God is the Devil's favorite weapon! And, it will be seven times worse than it was before. That is because you will know that you tried to get rid of it and failed."

You may be thinking, "The Holy Spirit didn't say that to you. You just made that up." Well, I can understand why people would feel that way. But, I think that is because in our time we have such weak faith that most people think it is unusual or even impossible for the Holy Spirit to send messages to people. But, I think the Holy Spirit is willing to speak to us all the time. All we have to do is to pray for Him to speak to us and then listen for his voice.

After this prayer, the meeting place shook, and they were all filled with the Holy Spirit. Then they preached the word of God with boldness.

Acts 4:31 (NLT)

Dear God, thank you for showing me the cause of my fear and how I can get rid of it. Now that I know these things, help me to put them into practice in my life right away, before the Devil brings them back and makes them worse. In Jesus' name, Amen

MESSAGE 24

How I Got to be a Christian

I have considered myself a Christian all my life, but I knew nothing about how I became entitled to be one. My perception of things was that Jews were the enemies of Christians during Jesus' time on earth; that Peter was a Catholic; that Paul was the first missionary; and that nobody knew who the first Gentile Christian was. So, I was surprised when I read the following scripture:

Then Jesus left Galilee and went north to the region of Tyre and Sidon. A Gentile woman who lived there came to Him, pleading, "Have mercy on me, O Lord, Son of David! For my daughter is possessed by a demon that torments her severely."

But Jesus gave her no reply, not even a word. Then,

his disciples urged Him to send her away. "Tell her to go away," they said. "She is bothering us with all her begging."

Then Jesus said to the woman, "I was sent only to help God's lost sheep—the people of Israel."

But she came and worshipped Him, pleading again, "Lord, help me!"

Jesus responded, "It isn't good to take food from the children and throw it to the dogs."

She replied, "That's true, Lord, but even dogs are allowed to eat the scraps that fall beneath their master's table."

"Dear woman," Jesus said to her, "your faith is great. Your request is granted." And her daughter was instantly healed.

Matthew 15:21-28 (NLT)

My first reaction when I read this was to be surprised that Jesus only came to earth to save the Jews. That hurt me, but I had to face the fact He did not come to save Gentiles like me. (The word "Gentile" is defined as any person who is not Jewish.)

It is also important to note that while Jesus healed this woman's daughter, He did not forgive her sins or grant her salvation. That was just for the Jews.

After I found this out, I wanted to find out exactly what happened to allow Gentiles to become Christians. I found the answer in the following passage. It is very long, but it contains important information that I did not know before. Since I know that I am living in either "my" end times or "the" end times, I am much more willing to study long passages of scripture than I was when I was young.

In Caesarea there lived a Roman army officer named Cornelius, who was a captain of the Italian Regiment.

He was a devout, God-fearing man, as was everyone in his household. He gave generously to the poor and prayed regularly to God. One afternoon about three o'clock, he had a vision in which he saw an angel of God coming toward him. "Cornelius!" the angel said.

Cornelius stared at him in terror. "What is it, sir?" he asked the angel.

And the angel replied, "Your prayers and gifts to the poor have been received by God as an offering! Now send some men to Joppa, and summon a man named Simon Peter. He is staying with Simon, a tanner who lives near the seashore."

As soon as the angel was gone, Cornelius called two of his household servants and a devout soldier, one of his personal attendants. He told them what had happened and sent them off to Joppa.

The next day as Cornelius's messengers were nearing the town, Peter went up on the flat roof to pray.

It was about noon, and he was hungry. But while a meal was being prepared, he fell into a trance. He saw the sky open, and something like a large sheet was let down by its four corners. In the sheet were all sorts of animals, reptiles, and birds. Then a voice said to him, "Get up, Peter; kill and eat them."

"No, Lord," Peter declared. "I have never eaten anything that our Jewish laws have declared impure and unclean."

But the voice spoke again: "Do not call something unclean if God has made it clean." The same vision was repeated three times. Then the sheet was suddenly pulled up to Heaven.

Peter was very perplexed. What could the vision mean? Just then the men sent by Cornelius found Simon's house. Standing outside the gate, they asked if a man named Simon Peter was staying there.

Meanwhile, as Peter was puzzling over the vision,

the Holy Spirit said to him, "Three men have come looking for you. Get up, go downstairs, and go with them without hesitation. Don't worry, for I have sent them."

So Peter went down and said, "I'm the man you are looking for. Why have you come?"

They said, "We were sent by Cornelius, a Roman officer. He is a devout and God-fearing man, well respected by all the Jews. A holy angel instructed him to summon you to his house so that he can hear your message." So Peter invited the men to stay for the night. The next day he went with them, accompanied by some of the brothers from Joppa.

They arrived in Caesarea the following day. Cornelius was waiting for them and had called together his relatives and close friends. As Peter entered his home, Cornelius fell at his feet and worshipped him. But Peter pulled him up and said, "Stand up! I'm a human being *just like you!" So they talked together and went inside, where many others were assembled.*

Peter told them, "You know it is against our laws for a Jewish man to enter a Gentile home like this or to associate with you. But God has shown me that I should no longer think of anyone as impure or unclean. So I came without objection as soon as I was sent for. Now tell me why you sent for me."

Cornelius replied, "Four days ago I was praying in my house about this same time, three o'clock in the afternoon. Suddenly, a man in dazzling clothes was standing in front of me. He told me, 'Cornelius, your prayer has been heard, and your gifts to the poor have been noticed by God! Now send messengers to Joppa, and summon a man named Simon Peter. He is staying in the home of Simon, a tanner who lives near the seashore.' So I sent for you at once, and it was good of you to come.

Now, we are all here, waiting before God to hear the message the Lord has given you."

Then Peter replied, "I see very clearly that God shows no favoritism. In every nation He accepts those who fear him and do what is right. This is the message of Good News for the people of Israel—that there is peace with God through Jesus Christ, who is Lord of all. You know what happened throughout Judea, beginning in Galilee, after John began preaching his message of baptism. And you know that God anointed Jesus of Nazareth with the Holy Spirit and with power. Then, Jesus went around doing good and healing all who were oppressed by the devil, for God was with Him.

"And we apostles are witnesses of all He did throughout Judea and in Jerusalem. They put Him to death by hanging Him on a cross, but God raised Him to on the third day. Then God allowed Him to appear, not to the general public, but to us whom God had chosen *in advance to be his witnesses. We were those who ate and drank with Him after He rose from the dead. And He ordered us to preach everywhere and to testify that Jesus is the one appointed by God to be the judge of all— the living and the dead. He is the one all the prophets testified about, saying that everyone who believes in Him will have their sins forgiven through his name."*

Even as Peter was saying these things, the Holy Spirit fell upon all who were listening to the message. The Jewish believers who came with Peter were amazed that the gift of the Holy Spirit had been poured out on the Gentiles, too. For they heard them speaking in other tongues and praising God.

Then Peter asked, "Can anyone object to them being baptized, now that they have received the Holy Spirit just as we did?" So he gave orders for them to be baptized in the name of Jesus Christ. Afterward Cornelius asked him to stay with them for several days.

Acts 10:1-48 (NLT)

So, let me correct my assumptions.

While some Jews were opponents of Christians during Jesus' time on earth, all Christians were Jews.

Peter was both a Jew and the founder of the Catholic Church.

Paul was not the first missionary, Peter was.

It is specified in the Bible that the first Gentile Christian was a man named Cornelius.

It is clear to me that Jesus did not come into the world to save everybody. He came into the world to save only the Jews. So, what changed this plan?

The first thing that caused Jesus to even talk to a Gentile was His experience with the Gentile woman who asked Him to heal her daughter. Jesus told her that it was the greatness of her faith that caused Him to grant her request that her daughter be healed by Him. It seems to me that He was also very impressed by her humility.

In the case of Cornelius, the Bible said that God was impressed by the fact that Cornelius gave generously to the poor and prayed regularly to God.

So, I am entitled to become a Christian because God was impressed by four things that two Gentiles did.

- Having faith in God
- Having humility towards God
- Giving generously to the poor
- Praying regularly

Faith. Humility. Giving. Praying. These are the things that impressed God so much that he allowed Gentiles like me to become Christians. I need to remember those four words every day.

I now realize that I, as a Gentile, am an immigrant into Christianity. I also realize that for me as a Gentile, being allowed to become a Christian is a privilege that was given to me, not a right that I inherited.

Dear God, Help me to remember that it was having faith in you, being humble towards you, praying regularly to you, and giving generously to the poor that impressed you enough to let Gentiles become Christians. In Jesus name, Amen

MESSAGE 25

The Father and The Son

When I was young and healthy and had a job, I read the Bible almost every day. But, I read it very superficially. I usually just read a one page devotional out of a devotional book that had one devotional for every day in the year. That took me about ten minutes a day.

There were a few years when I got a little more ambitious than that. During those times, I went from Genesis to Revelation, reading a chapter a day. I underlined verses that spoke to me and made notes in the margins of the Bible about what I got out of each chapter I read and the verses I underlined. This took me about twenty minutes a day. It was better than reading one page from a devotional book, but it was still a helter-skelter way to study the Bible. When I did that, I thought I was doing a really good job of studying the Bible. But, I now know I was wrong, because I did not learn anything that I still remember today by doing that. Good Bible study always teaches us things that we never forget.

I never before did Bible study like I'm doing it now. I now start off with a question to which I do not know the answer. Then, I spend an average of three or four hours studying the entire Bible to look for an answer to that question.

I changed to this more in depth method of studying the Bible because, as I got old and developed Parkinsonism, I realized that my opportunity to study the Bible was not going to last too much longer. I knew that I needed to take the Bible and Christianity a lot more seriously. I wanted to get as much understanding of Christianity as I could in order to build up my faith as quickly as possible.

When selecting a topic to study, I think of something that I know is important to Christianity, but which I do not understand. Today's message is about one of those subjects. Is Jesus the Son equal in authority to God the Father?

For some reason, I always assumed they were the same entity in different forms. I thought they had equal authority. However, the following verses changed my mind.

So Jesus explained, "I tell you the truth, the Son can do nothing by Himself. He does only what He sees the Father doing. Whatever the Father does, the Son also does. For the Father loves the Son and shows Him everything He is doing. In fact, the Father will show Him how to do even greater works than healing this man. Then you will truly be astonished. For just as the Father gives life to those He raises from the dead, so the Son gives life to anyone He wants. In addition, the Father judges no one. Instead, He has given the Son absolute power to judge, so that everyone will honor the Son, just as they honor the Father. Anyone who does not honor the Son is certainly not honoring the Father who sent Him."

John 5:19-23 (NLT)

This passage certainly makes me think that Jesus is under the authority of God the Father, and not equal in authority to Him. Jesus says that He can do nothing by Himself. Jesus also says that He can only do what He does because God the Father has given Him the authority to do it. This is the kind of relationship that I would expect to see between a son, who goes to work for his father in his father's business, and his father.

Here are some other scriptures that led me to the same conclusion.

"Who are you?" they demanded.

Jesus replied, "The one I have always claimed to be. I have much to say about you and much to condemn, but I won't. For I say only what I have heard from the one who sent me, and He is completely truthful." But they still didn't understand that He was talking about his Father.

So Jesus said, "When you have lifted up The Son of Man on the cross, then you will understand that I am He. I do nothing on my own but say only what the Father taught me. And the one who sent me is with me—He has not deserted me. For I always do what pleases Him."

John 8:25-29 (NLT)

"Remember what I told you: I am going away, but I

will come back to you again. If you really loved me, you would be happy that I am going to the Father, who is greater than I am."

John 14:28 (NLT)

"However, no one knows the day or hour when these things will happen, not even the angels in Heaven or the Son himself. Only the Father knows."

Matthew 24:36 (NLT)

"Why ask me about what is good?" Jesus replied. "There is only one who is good."

Matthew 19:17 (NLT)

"However, those the Father has given me will come to me, and I will never reject them. For I have come down from Heaven to do the will of God who sent me, not to do my own will. And this is the will of God, that

I should not lose even one of all those He has given me, but that I should raise them up at the last day. For it is my Father's will that all who see his son and believe in Him should have eternal life. I will raise them up at the last day."

John 6:37–40 (NLT)

He walked away, about a stone's throw, and knelt down and prayed. "Father, if you are willing, please take this cup of suffering away from me. Yet I want your will to be done, not mine."

Luke 22:41–42 (NLT)

Jesus said, "Father, forgive them, for they don't know what they are doing."

Luke 23:34 (NLT)

At about three o'clock, Jesus called out with a loud voice, "Eli, Eli, lema sabachthani?" which means, "My God, My God, why have you abandoned me?"

Matthew 27:46 (NLT)

"Why do you call me good?" Jesus asked. "Only God is truly good."

Mark 10:18 (NLT) and Luke 18:19 (NLT)

Jesus told them, "If God were your Father, you would love me, because I have come to you from God. I am not here on my own, but He sent me."

John 8:42 (NLT)

Jesus answered, "If I want glory for myself, it doesn't count. But it is my Father who will glorify me. You say, 'He is our God,' but you don't even know Him. I know

Him. If I said otherwise, I would be as great a liar as you! But I do know Him and obey Him."

John 8:54-55 (NLT)

Based on the scriptures quoted above, I believe that Jesus the Son is under the authority of God the Father. However, there are many things that I do not know. You may disagree with me, and you may be right.

The purpose of this book is not to assert that my conclusions are correct. The purpose of this book is to share a method of Bible study that has brought me closer to God.

Serious Bible study is an acknowledgement of God. And that acknowledgement is a form of worship, which God always respects and appreciates.

Dear God, Thank you for giving me questions and for also giving me a way to seek answers to them. Doing this helps me feel closer to you. In Jesus' name, Amen

MESSAGE 26

What I Need

On the day of Pentecost all the believers were meeting together in one place. Suddenly, there was a sound from Heaven like the roaring of a mighty windstorm, and it filled the house where they were sitting. Then, what looked like flames or tongues of fire appeared and settled on each of them. And everyone present was filled with the Holy Spirit and began speaking in other languages, as the Holy Spirit gave them this ability.

At that time there were devout Jews from every nation living in Jerusalem. When they heard the loud noise, everyone came running, and they were bewildered to hear their own languages being spoken by the believers.

They were completely amazed. "How can this be?"

they exclaimed. "These people are all from Galilee, and yet we hear them speaking in our own native languages! Here we are—Parthians, Medes, Elamites, people from Mesopotamia, Judea, Cappadocia, Pontus, the province of Asia, Phrygia, Pamphylia, Egypt, and the areas of Libya around Cyrene, visitors from Rome (both Jews and converts to Judaism), Cretans, and Arabs. And we all hear these people speaking in our own languages about the wonderful things God has done!" They stood there amazed and perplexed. "What can this mean?" they asked each other.

But others in the crowd ridiculed them, saying, "They're just drunk, that's all!"

Then Peter stepped forward with the eleven other apostles and shouted to the crowd. "Listen carefully, all of you, fellow Jews and residents of Jerusalem! Make no mistake about this. These people are not drunk, as some of you are assuming. Nine o'clock in the morning is much too early for that. No, what you see was predicted long ago by the prophet Joel:

"'In the last days,' God says, 'I will pour out my Spirit upon all people. Your sons and daughters will prophesy. Your young men will see visions, and your old men will dream dreams. In those days I will pour out my Spirit even on my servants—men and women alike— and they will prophesy. And I will cause wonders in the heavens above and signs on the earth below—blood and fire and clouds of smoke. The sun will become dark, and the moon will turn blood red before that great and glorious day of the Lord arrives. But everyone who calls on the name of the Lord will be saved.'

"People of Israel, listen! God publicly endorsed Jesus the Nazarene by doing powerful miracles, wonders, and signs through Him, as you well know. But God knew what would happen, and his prearranged plan was carried out when Jesus was betrayed. With the help of

lawless Gentiles, you nailed Him to a cross and killed Him. But God released Him from the horrors of death and raised Him back to life, for death could not keep Him in its grip."

Acts 2:1-24 (NLT)

Those who believed what Peter said were baptized and added to the church that day—about 3,000 in all.

All the believers devoted themselves to the apostles' teaching, and to the fellowship, and to sharing in meals (including the Lord's Supper), and to prayer.

A deep sense of awe came over them all, and the apostles performed many miraculous signs and wonders. And all the believers met together in one place and shared everything they had. They sold their property and possessions and shared the money with those in need.

They worshipped together at the Temple each day, met in homes for the Lord's Supper, and shared their

meals with great joy and generosity—all while praising
God and enjoying the goodwill of all the people. And
each day the Lord added to their fellowship those who
were being saved.

Acts 2:41-47 (NLT)

I used to wonder how Christianity spread from just
a few people in Jerusalem to become a religion with
many churches on many street corners in small towns
and big cities all over the world. Well, this scripture
explains how that happened. To me, one word sums
it up: commitment.

These passages describe the first Christian church
service in history and the beginning of the Christian
religion.

Have you ever been to a church service anything like
the one described in this passage? Have you ever been
to a church service where everybody put everything

they had in the collection plate? Have you ever been to a church service where the congregation witnessed God performing brand new miracles, instead of just listening to somebody talk about miracles that God performed thousands of years ago?

The closest thing to it that I have ever seen were the Billy Graham crusades our family watched on TV when I was growing up. We would sit around the television and watch them. The Holy Spirit was in those crusade meetings. You can still watch them on YouTube and feel the presence of the Holy Spirit right through the television. The wonderful hymns sung by Cliff Barrows and the crusade choir, the special music by George Beverly Shea, the musical testimonies by guests like Stuart Hamblen singing "It is No Secret What God Can Do," and the unequivocal messages by Billy Graham all made these meetings extremely special. You could feel the strong presence of the Holy Spirit in those services.

Back then, I got an allowance of one dollar a week. Every month, I put a one dollar bill and one penny in an envelope, addressed it to "Billy Graham, Minneapolis, Minnesota," and faithfully put it in the mail. Trust me, only the Holy Spirit could cause a little boy to part with over 25% of his allowance!

I know for a fact that we are living in the end times. It might be the end times when Jesus returns to earth, or it might be the end times when we leave earth by dying. But, either way, we will all be seeing Jesus soon.

We need to invite the Holy Spirit to take over our lives. We need the feelings the people got at that first Christian church service described in the Bible. We need to feel the presence of God, the way my family felt it watching those old Billy Graham crusades.

Without the presence of the Holy Spirit, there is

no salvation in Christianity. It is just a nice philosophy for living on earth and nothing more. But with the presence of the Holy Spirit, Christianity is entirely different. It is a living connection to God that can forgive sins, produce miracles, answer prayers, and save us when we die.

Dear God, Thank you for making the Holy Spirit available to me. I need to feel your presence, not just talk about your philosophy. In Jesus name, Amen

MESSAGE 27

Spiritual Gifts

There are different kinds of spiritual gifts, but the same Spirit is the source of them all. There are different kinds of service, but we serve the same Lord. God works in different ways, but it is the same God who does the work in all of us.

A spiritual gift is given to each of us so we can help each other. To one person the Spirit gives the ability to give wise advice; to another the same Spirit gives a message of special knowledge. The same Spirit gives great faith to another, and to someone else the one Spirit gives the gift of healing. He gives one person the power to perform miracles, and another the ability to prophesy. He gives someone else the ability to discern whether a message is from the Spirit of God or from another spirit.

Still another person is given the ability to speak in unknown languages, while another is given the ability to interpret what is being said. It is the one and only Spirit who distributes all these gifts. He alone decides which gift each person should have.

1 Corinthians 12:4-11 (NLT)

For me, personally, this is one of the greatest, most encouraging, and most comforting passages in the entire Bible. Let me tell you what God has shown me about it that has me so excited.

To begin with, it tells exactly why we are all given spiritual gifts. It says, "A spiritual gift is given to each of us so we can help each other."

So, if I think I have a spiritual gift but I am not using it to help other Christians, I need to start using my spiritual gift to help other Christians. That's why God gave it to me.

I think that I might have the spiritual gift of giving a message of special knowledge. So, I am writing these messages with the sole purpose of helping other Christians by sharing these messages with them.

As I have been writing these messages, I thought the things I have written in them came to me from the Holy Spirit and would help other Christians. But, there were many times when I told my wife, "Why would God give these messages to me? I don't even have very strong faith." This knowledge of my limitations and weaknesses really made me wonder if I wasn't being hypocritical to think that a person like me could possibly have anything of use to other Christians, especially those who are so much better Christians than I am.

But, God answered that concern for me in this passage. In the discussion of spiritual gifts in this passage, it says, "The same Spirit gives great faith to another." So, I should not be surprised that my faith is not as great as the faith of some other people. The people who have been given greater faith than I have may not have been given a message of special knowledge, which I believe is my spiritual gift.

It's as if we were trying to build a house. We would need all types of people: carpenters, plumbers, electricians, painters and roofers, just to name a few. Without using our individual gifts together, we could not build a house. If everybody in our group was an electrician, we could not build a house. We would need everybody's special gifts to build a house.

There is something else I feel led to say. This passage does not list all the spiritual gifts. There are many more. One is the ability to succeed in business and wisely accumulate money, like the women in the

Bible who provided the financial support needed by Jesus and His disciples. Another is the ability that God gave people like Bill and Gloria Gaither to write wonderful gospel music.

I think gospel music serves the same purpose today that speaking in tongues served in New Testament time. I think the Holy Spirit uses gospel music to reach our emotions, which is just as important as other spiritual gifts that are intended to reach our minds.

But, if Bill and Gloria Gaither wrote their beautiful gospel music and just sang it around their home, they would be failing. It was given to them to use to help other Christians.

The same is true of Christians who have been given other spiritual gifts. If they just use them for themselves, they are failing. God wants us all to use our spiritual gifts to help other Christians.

Dear God, Thank you for the lessons you have

taught me about spiritual gifts. Please use these messages to help other Christians receive the same encouragement from reading them that I have received from writing them. In Jesus' name, Amen

MESSAGE 28

Why Moses couldn't Enter
the Promised Land

I have been trying very hard to get this book published. A few weeks ago, a good friend of mine, who has helped and encouraged me many times, asked me to send him three printed copies. He said he was going to give them to some people to read. My friend and I hoped that one of them might like this book and help us get it published.

After I gave my friend the printed copies, I was very hopeful that there would be some progress towards getting this published. Every day, I would get up and hope I would hear from my friend. But, about a week went by without my friend contacting me. I prayed and asked God what I should do. Then, an idea about what to do came to me. I thought it was an answer to my prayer for guidance. I wrote my friend a message about it. But, after several weeks, I had not heard from my friend.

This caused me to get very discouraged. A couple of days later, I told my wife about this. As I was talking with her, a thought came into my head. It was, "Find out why Moses did not get to enter the Promised Land." I thought that God had put this thought in my head, so I immediately looked this up. This is what I found:

There was no water for the people to drink at that place, so they rebelled against Moses and Aaron. The people blamed Moses and said, "If only we had died in the Lord's presence with our brothers! Why have you brought the congregation of the Lord's people into this wilderness to die, along with all our livestock? Why did you make us leave Egypt and bring us here to this terrible place? This land has no grain, no figs, no grapes, no pomegranates, and no water to drink!"

Moses and Aaron turned away from the people and went to the entrance of the Tabernacle, where they fell face down on the ground. Then the glorious presence of the Lord appeared to them, and the Lord said to Moses, "You and Aaron must take the staff and assemble the entire community. As the people watch, speak to the rock over there, and it will pour out its water. You will provide enough water from the rock to satisfy the whole community and their livestock."

So Moses did as he was told. He took the staff from the place where it was kept before the Lord. Then he and Aaron summoned the people to come and gather at the rock. "Listen, you rebels!" he shouted. "Must we bring you water from this rock?" Then Moses raised his hand and struck the rock twice with the staff, and water gushed out. So the entire community and their livestock drank their fill.

But the Lord said to Moses and Aaron, "Because you did not trust me enough to demonstrate my holiness to the people of Israel, you will not lead them into the land I am giving them!"

Numbers 20:2-12 (NLT)

After I read this, I still did not see what Moses had done wrong. Then, when I read it again, I found what I had been looking for! God had told Moses to only speak to the rock to make it produce water. But, Moses had not trusted God enough to do that. Instead, Moses hit the rock two times with his staff.

When He first called Moses, God had told him how to use that staff.

But Moses protested again, "What if they won't

believe me or listen to me? What if they say, 'The Lord never appeared to you'?"

Then the Lord asked him, "What is that in your hand?"

"A shepherd's staff," Moses replied.

"Throw it down on the ground," the Lord told him. So Moses threw down the staff, and it turned into a snake! Moses jumped back.

Then the Lord told him, "Reach out and grab its tail." So Moses reached out and grabbed it, and it turned back into a shepherd's staff in his hand.

"Perform this sign," the Lord told him. "Then they will believe that the Lord, the God of their ancestors— the God of Abraham, the God of Isaac, and the God of Jacob—really has appeared to you."

Exodus 4:1-5 (NLT)

After that, God told Moses to use that staff many

times to perform miracles. Instead of summarizing these descriptions of how God told Moses to use that staff, I am including the full scriptures, because they show how much power God put into that staff. They make it easy to see how Moses came to rely so much on that staff.

So Moses took his wife and sons, put them on a donkey, and headed back to the land of Egypt. In his hand he carried the staff of God.

Exodus 4:20 (NLT)

Then the Lord said to Moses and Aaron, "Pharaoh will demand, 'Show me a miracle.' When he does this, say to Aaron, 'Take your staff and throw it down in front of Pharaoh, and it will become a serpent.'"

So Moses and Aaron went to Pharaoh and did what the Lord had commanded them. Aaron threw down his staff before Pharaoh and his officials and it became a serpent!

Exodus 7:8-10 (NLT)

Then the Lord said to Moses, "Pharaoh's heart is stubborn, and he still refuses to let the people go. So go to Pharaoh in the morning as he goes down to the river. Stand on the bank of the Nile and meet him there. Be sure to take along the staff that turned into a snake. Then announce to him, 'The Lord, the God of the Hebrews, has sent me to tell you, "Let my people go, so they can worship me in the wilderness." Until now, you have refused to listen to Him. So this is what the Lord says: "I will show you that I am the Lord." Look! I will strike the water of the Nile with this staff in my hand, and the river will turn to blood. The fish in it will die, and the river will stink. The Egyptians will not be able to drink any water from the Nile.'"

Then the Lord said to Moses: "Tell Aaron, 'Take your staff and raise your hand over the waters of Egypt—all its rivers, canals, ponds, and all the reservoirs. Turn all the water to blood. Everywhere in Egypt the water will turn to blood, even the water stored in wooden bowls and stone pots.'"

So Moses and Aaron did just as the Lord commanded them. As Pharaoh and all of his officials watched, Aaron raised his staff and struck the water of the Nile. Suddenly, the whole river turned to blood! The fish in the river died, and the water became so foul that the Egyptians couldn't drink it. There was blood everywhere throughout the land of Egypt.

Exodus 7:14-21 (NLT)

Then the Lord said to Moses, "Tell Aaron, 'Raise the staff in your hand over all the rivers, canals, and ponds of Egypt, and bring up frogs over all the land.'"

So Aaron raised his hand over the waters of Egypt, and frogs came up and covered the whole land!

Exodus 8:5-6 (NLT)

So the Lord said to Moses, "Tell Aaron, 'Raise your staff and strike the ground. The dust will turn into swarms of gnats throughout the land of Egypt.'" So Moses and Aaron did just as the Lord had commanded them. When Aaron raised his hand and struck the ground with his staff, gnats infested the entire land, covering the Egyptians and their animals. All the dust in the land of Egypt turned into gnats.

Exodus 8:16-17 (NLT)

Then the Lord said to Moses, "Lift your hand toward the sky so hail may fall on the people, the livestock, and all the plants throughout the land of Egypt."

So Moses lifted his staff toward the sky, and the Lord

sent thunder and hail, and lightning flashed toward the earth. The Lord sent a tremendous hailstorm against all the land of Egypt. Never in all the history of Egypt had there been a storm like that, with such devastating hail and continuous lightning. It left all of Egypt in ruins. The hail struck down everything in the open field— people, animals, and plants alike. Even the trees were destroyed. The only place without hail was the region of Goshen, where the people of Israel lived.

Exodus 9:22-26 (NLT)

Then the Lord said to Moses, "Raise your hand over the land of Egypt to bring on the locusts. Let them cover the land and devour every plant that survived the hailstorm."

So Moses raised his staff over Egypt, and the Lord caused an east wind to blow over the land all that day and through the night. When morning arrived, the east wind had brought the locusts. And the locusts swarmed over the whole land of Egypt, settling in dense swarms from one end of the country to the other. It was the worst locust plague in Egyptian history, and there has never been another one like it. For the locusts covered the whole country and darkened the land. They devoured every plant in the fields and all the fruit on the trees that had survived the hailstorm. Not a single leaf was left on the trees and plants throughout the land of Egypt.

Exodus 10:12-15 (NLT)

Then the Lord said to Moses, "Why are you crying out to me? Tell the people to get moving! Pick up your staff and raise your hand over the sea. Divide the water so the Israelites can walk through the middle of the sea on dry ground."

Exodus 14:15-16 (NLT)

The Lord said to Moses, "Walk out in front of the people. Take your staff, the one you used when you struck the water of the Nile, and call some of the elders of Israel to join you. I will stand before you on the rock at Mount Sinai. Strike the rock, and water will come gushing out. Then the people will be able to drink." So Moses struck the rock as he was told, and water gushed out as the elders looked on.

Exodus 17:5-6 (NLT)

While the people of Israel were still at Rephidim, the warriors of Amalek attacked them. Moses commanded Joshua, "Choose some men to go out and fight the army of Amalek for us. Tomorrow, I will stand at the top of the hill, holding the staff of God in my hand."

So Joshua did what Moses had commanded and fought the army of Amalek. Meanwhile, Moses, Aaron, and Hur climbed to the top of a nearby hill. As long as

Moses held up the staff in his hand, the Israelites had the advantage. But whenever he dropped his hand, the Amalekites gained the advantage.

Exodus 17:8-11 (NLT)

God had used that staff to bless Moses with the power to accomplish miracles. But, over time, Moses had come to rely on that staff instead of relying on God, who had made the staff so powerful. So, when God told Moses to speak to the rock to make water come forth, Moses did not trust God enough to do what God told him to do. Instead, Moses relied on that staff and struck the rock with it two times. Because of all the times that God had used that staff to help him, Moses could not help himself from relying on that staff. He should have relied only on God, without whom that staff would have never had any power.

When I read this, I knew exactly what God was

telling me. God had put my friend in my life and used my friend to help me, just like God had used that staff to help Moses. But, like Moses, I had come to rely on my friend instead of relying on God. I had forgotten that without God I would have never met my friend, and my friend would have never been touched by God to help me. The gift can never be greater than the giver.

Dear God, Please forgive me for relying on my friend. Help me to always rely only on you, and to never rely on any of the people or things you have put in my life to bless me. In Jesus' name, Amen

Printed in the United States
by Baker & Taylor Publisher Services